THE WAY OF THE GOLFER
Searching For New Horizons

By

Edward A. Tischler

authorHOUSE®

AuthorHouse™
1663 Liberty Drive
Bloomington, IN 47403
www.authorhouse.com
Phone: 1-800-839-8640

First published by AuthorHouse   05/26/2011

ISBN: 978-1-4634-1485-6 (sc)
ISBN: 978-1-4634-1490-0 (ebk)
ISBN: 978-1-4634-4466-2 (hc)

Printed in the United States of America

Any people depicted in stock imagery provided by Thinkstock are models, and such images are being used for illustrative purposes only.
Certain stock imagery © Thinkstock.

This book is printed on acid-free paper.

Table of Contents

Foreword –   *f.1*

Introduction –   *i.1*

Chapter One – The Player's First Experience   **1**
The Golfing Journey

Chapter Two – Awareness Imagery, & Coaching   **7**
The Role Of Imagery
The Game: Mental or Physical?
The Way We Learn Imagery
The Role Of The Coach
Awareness & The Way We Learn
The Performance Mode
Golf Is An Underhanded Game
Tossing Is Natural
Clubface Awareness
Using Your Natural Hand
From Short Game To Long Game
Awareness Skills
The Process Of Imagery
Watch Out For Negative Images
Staying Within Yourself

Chapter Three – Playing The Game   43

Why Do We Play Games?
Analyst, Hoper, Or Golfer?
The Purpose vs. The Goal
Spending Time Purposefully
Who Do You Bring To The Course?

Chapter Four – Golf Is A Target Sport   59

Developing The Fundamentals
Golf Is A Target Sport
Tossing It Around
Develop Tossing Awareness
Tossing With The Club
Playing The Shots
Extending Your Follow-Through
Developing Short Game Confidence
Summary Of The Fundamental Short Game Skills

Chapter Five – Beyond The Short Game   99

Beginning With The Finish
The Fundamentals & The Finish
Developing The Finish
Journeying To The Finish
Develop A Centered Swing
Pivoting & Finishing
Understand The Lateral Shift
The Swinging Motion
Turning On The Power
Setting It All In Motion
Summary Of The Fundamental Long Game Skills

Chapter Six – Fine Tuning Your Skills　　　143
Finding The Source

Chapter Seven – Maintaining Your Skills　　　153
The Warm-up Routine
One-handed Tossing
Two-Handed Tossing
Swing-Tossing
The Short Game The Warm-Up Routine
Finishing The Swing
Swinging To The Finish
Turning To The Finish
Fine-Tuning Your Skills
The Warm-up Routine Summary

Chapter Eight – Know Your Inner Golfer　　　165
Letting Your Inner Golfer Play
The Game

Chapter Nine – The Future Of The Game　　　179
Golf, An Ever-Evolving Game

Chapter Ten – The Photo Album　　　191

ACKNOWLEDGEMENTS

I would like to give the following people special thanks for the inspiration, insight, and guidance their presence and efforts have provided throughout my life and career. All their contributions have had a direct influence on what I've expressed within this book:

To my coach and friend, Fred Shoemaker, whose inspiration has provided a beacon of enlightenment within my game and life. Throughout our friendship he has continually opened my awareness to the possibility of an extraordinary way of living life.

To Michael Murphy and Timothy Gallwey for providing us all with their books Golf In The Kingdom and The Inner Game Of Golf. Their works have provided tremendous insights into the nature of the game we dream of playing. With the introduction of their approaches into my life, my game has always journeyed down a path that has been anything but traditional and ordinary.

To my friend Larry Miller for writing the foreword to this book, and committing much time and energy practicing the path of The Way Of The Golfer.

To my Father, for setting a good example for me to follow. In doing so, he introduced me to the game while instilling in me patience, etiquette, sportsmanship, and a true love for the game.

To My mother and the rest of my family for helping me forge through the trying times in my career.

To all my students who have taken an interest in the Way of New Horizons Golf. For they have all helped illuminate the subtleties which define the way. Without their efforts, the New Horizons approach could have never been made complete.

NEW HORIZONS GOLF

A JOURNEY INTO THE EXPERIENCE

"THE GOLFER'S FUTURE IS INEVITABLY FULL OF ANTICIPATION. FOR IN THE FUTURE THE POSSIBILITY EXISTS THAT THE SWING, THE BALL, AND THE TARGET WILL ALL MEET WITHIN ONE MAJESTIC MOMENT."

Foreword

For several decades golf instruction has remained stagnant, as evidenced by the fact that the average handicap has not been lowered—despite advances in golf club technology and improvements in course conditions.

This stagnation is not due to a lack of knowledge of swing mechanics by instructors—quite the contrary. Video technology has enabled teachers to isolate quite precisely the proven effective mechanics of the golf swing. Almost every trained instructor knows the way a good, effective golf swing works.

The problem has been a lack of innovation in the *communication* arena. The game has not had enough creative, imaginative teachers who discover new ways to explain the *known* mechanics to students in ways that enable them to perform those mechanics.

But all that has quickly changed. Led by the pioneer thinking of Michael Murphy, an army of forward thinking, innovative teachers have mobilized around the world, and are poised to revolutionize the way the game is taught and learned.

The vanguard of this instructional revolution—

imaginative instructors like Fred Shoemaker ("Extraordinary Golf"), myself with "Holographic Golf" & "Beyond Golf", and other—is pushing ever forward, and the evolution of golf instruction is accelerating. The movement is snowballing as creative teachers with ideas once considered esoteric are coming forth with innovations *that work.*

With "The Way Of The Golfer", Ed Tischler not only joins this vanguard, but he moves to the front of the movement with a structured method of learning that combines the *"best of the best".*

Ed's book is a good example of the power of a new perspective. "The Way Of The Golfer" proves that if you stay on path, you'll find the way. His book is the best delineation of the most effective path to better and enjoyable golf that I've seen.

Most books (on most any subject involving self-improvement) speak volumes on the desired end-result. But they fall short when it comes down to the *how* of reaching that result.

The "Way Of The Golfer" is filled with innovative, creative methods which enable the average golfer to experience the magnificence of well-executed golf shots, and it is filled with structured drills which enhance the golfer's ability to repeat those shots consistently.

f.2

Every golfer, from beginner to touring professional, can improve and develop as a golfer by studiously committing to Ed's methods. *"The Way Of The Golfer"* takes golf's new instructional direction to yet another level, and further contributes to the end of instructional stagnation.

Larry Miller, P.G.A. member
Former PGA Tour Player, author of
"Holographic Golf" and *"Beyond Golf"*,
Member, Golf Writer Ass'n of America

Introduction

As I began writing this book, my main intention was to present readers with the basic information we use in the *New Horizons Golf Approach*. My goal was to produce a sort of textbook that our students could use during their training. Thus, if they ever found themselves off track, they'd have some reference material to fall back on. I also wanted to introduce this material in such a way that anyone could benefit from reading it, even if they had never attended one of our training courses. My hope is that this book will help you develop a very productive approach to your game.

For that to come true, I believe we must reach a meeting of our minds, a sort of intellectual contract, based on my commitment as a dedicated coach and yours as an honorable student. My commitments are to provide you with the necessary information to make your new approach productive in the areas of learning, enjoyment, and performance. Your commitments involve sticking with the program and dedicating the necessary time until you truly understand what it can do for you.

The *New Horizons Approach* is much different from any traditional ones you might know. It focuses on *awareness* as the natural path to learning. It deals with your inner relations as well as your physical ones. So, you will get to know the *inner you* while developing your outer foundation. It involves the possibility that you already possess a truly magnificent game of golf. You simply need to express it. Along the way you will learn how to quiet your mind and relax your body. Like any athletic endeavor, you will establish the necessary physical skills, however, you will also come to understand the necessary inner skills. In short, you will find a true balance between mind and body. So, you will come to understand the workings of your inner golfer as well as your physical technique.

Completing the New Horizons training is certain to provide you with the skills, understanding, and motivation to maintain your way. As you learn from *The Way of the Golfer*, you'll develop the trust and confidence you have always believed possible. You will acquire a new perspective, one that will allow you to use your imagination to play the game. Along the way, your imagination will become free to direct your desires, instead of just dream about them.

Finally, you will develop such a thorough understanding of the game that you will be able to take your game to its next horizon.

Staying on path as a New Horizons Golfer will take commitment and stick-to-it-tiveness. It will require regular practice, and continual recommitment. It will require that you condition yourself physically, mentally, and inwardly. To truly find out want this journey has to offer, you must make the commitment to give *The Way of the Golfer* an honest try.

If you stick with the program continually, you will understand why your shots go where they go, and you'll understand how to target your play. You'll understand the game's true fundamentals, and the essence of how you play your shots. You'll truly know how to play the game, a game in which every shot is played as an expression of your inner desire.

Chapter One
A Player's First Experience

The Golfing Journey

Those who experience this mystical lure encounter a sense of fulfillment, belonging, and incommunicable happiness. Once experienced, there inevitably begins a search for the secret of mastering its execution. Furthermore, each player soon realizes it is because of this *mystical connexion* that he's attracted to the game in the first place. This is evident as we commonly experience the one shot per round that keeps us coming back.

As the player sets forth on this journey, there is always a question of where, and how, to begin. If you're one of the many who's searching for the answer to this question, then you need to understand how your approach to learning has a direct effect on your performance. In other words, you must become aware of your total approach to the game.

Your total approach consists of learning, performing, and maintaining the necessary skills and habits. Your learning depends on your skills of attention, awareness, and understanding. The quality of your performance depends on your powers of imagery, commitment, and trust. Your maintenance program involves routines for physical, mental, and inner conditioning. To play consistently, you must stay committed to your approach. It's an ongoing process, as long as you continue to play.

The success rate of the average golfer remains extremely low. For one thing, most golfers fail to truly pay attention to what they are doing as they practice and play. Instead of paying attention, they think too much. The more they think, the more confused they become, and the harder it is to pay attention. The confusion lies in the fact that there are many different viable ways to play. That's because golfers come in many different shapes and sizes. So, you must develop an approach that accommodates your particular needs. You must find a way of performing the fundamentals naturally.

Imagine this, as your body performs the fundamentals, it does so in your own unique way. As your body does so, your swing will take on a unique look. It will look unique because your body has unique features that are structurally different from all other golfers. Therefore, the way your body performs the fundamentals will have its own style.

If your fundamentals are sound, then your technique will be sound. This is true despite how unique your swing looks. To me, all swings on tour are unique. Even the players that have the same technical styles look uniquely different from each other. So, spend more time paying attention to your fundamentals than you do worrying about how your swing looks.

Notice that I said, "pay attention" to your fundamentals. This is because paying attention is more important than thinking. In many hours spent on the lesson tee, I've heard hundreds of students say, "I know what I am supposed to do, but I cannot do it." What they really mean is they know the concept of what they want to do, but are **unaware of how** to do it. The theories of physics or mechanics tell us what needs to happen, how we *let* it happen is another issue. Understanding the concept of what needs to happen involves thinking. Letting the action happen involves being aware. It involves paying attention to what is happening.

When you think about it, all those "how to" books out there are really "what needs to happen" books. *They assume we possess the basic skills necessary to perform the given tasks.* For example, how to books on carpentry assume you know how to hammer, saw, or use any other tool you need to build something. They never teach you how to hammer a nail or drill a hole. They assume you've already learned the basic skills through trial and error.

Finally, the essence of the game is simple, and the most simple view of the game is that you must become truly aware of your swing, the ball, and your target. If you do so, you will understand for yourself the best way of getting the ball in the hole. What I'm saying is that you learn through experience. And to learn through experience, you must pay attention to what you're doing. The more you pay attention to what you're doing, the more you'll become aware of what works, and the more you'll understand how to play great golf. Through this process of awareness you'll become absorbed in the very lure that attracts you to the game. Fascinated with this entire process, you'll find the courage to journey beyond the traditional barriers of the game, into a game with *new horizons.*

"Imagine this, as your body performs the fundamentals, it does so in your own unique way. As your body does so, your swing will take on a unique look. It will look unique because your body has unique features that are structurally different from all other golfers. Therefore, the way your body performs the fundamentals will have its own style."

Chapter Two
Imagery, Awareness, & Coaching

The Role Of Imagery

Imagery plays a critical role throughout every stage of your approach. While developing the proper skills, you'll spend a lot of time imagining what it is you want to happen. You'll also spend time searching for the most effective images. Once the proper skills are developed, you'll perform the skills by programming and reacting to the image of what you want to do. You must learn to trust the images to direct your performance.

I'd like to make a distinction between imagery and visualization. When you visualize something, you are simply creating a mental picture. When you imagine something, you also feel the sensations that relate to the mental picture. Think about it. When someone says *imagine* playing the perfect shot, what do you experience? When someone says visualize the perfect shot, what do you experience? We feel certain sensations when we imagine things, and we simply picture things when we visualize them. *Therefore, imagery is the combination of both visualization and sensitivity.*

I'm sure you've experienced a time when you imagined the shot you needed to play, and did it. This is often the case when putting well. You simply imagine the ball rolling down the line and into the hole. Then you react to the image, and roll the ball in the hole. You may also experience this occurrence when playing shots over bunkers or trees – you look up and naturally visualize the shot flying over the tree or sand trap. Then you add in the "feel," and your visualization is transformed into an image. Finally, you simply react to the image and play the shot. If you only visualize the shot, you're certain of what needs to happen, but your body fails to feel how to perform the shot.

If you *feel* what needs to happen, you will become aware of the total activity, and will experience confidence in your ability to perform the shot successfully. Once you combine your visualizations with the corresponding feel, you'll be certain of both what needs to happen, and how to perform what needs to happen. With such certainty comes confidence. When you possess confidence, you're destined to perform well.

You perform all your daily activities while engaged in that same process. When you drive your car, you imagine where you want to go. In this way you establish a destination, or target. Then you imagine the streets you need to travel, and the turns you need to make to get there. Thus, you've imagined a road map that directs your journey. Finally, you simply follow the image to your final destination. If you remain focused on the image, you'll travel directly to your final destination. However, if you become distracted, you may lose your way.

As we drive around town, we leave ourselves buffer zones between other cars. We expect obstacles to get in our way and slow us down. Even so, we are prepared to take alternate courses of action in case we get detoured by road construction, or accidents. Along the way, we constantly focus on our final destination. Doing so helps us to get there in a timely manner. Therefore, the more focused the image remains, the more likely your trips will avoid complications.

When you get distracted, you lose your way. You become frustrated, and you begin to feel rushed. You experience tension and anxiety, and you feel the need to make up for lost time. That's the same type of pressure you encounter on the golf course.

Conversely, when you stay focused on the golf course, you remain relaxed, and create clear images of the desired shots. You pay attention to what needs to happen, you pick a final destination for the shot, you imagine the path the ball needs to travel, and you feel the swing that will get the job done. Then you stay focused on the outward image. Remember, if you become distracted, you may lose your way.

Just as you leave yourself buffer zones when driving your car, you need to leave buffer zones on the golf course. Just as you're prepared for obstacles on the road, you need to be prepared for them on the golf course. Just as you plan alternate routes when you plan a trip, you need to plan for alternate routes on the golf course. Keep in mind that when things fail to work out smoothly you can still reach your final destination in a timely manner. You have to be flexible in your planning, and you need to allow for adaptations along the way. Therefore, choose your plans wisely, and be prepared for obstacles to get in the way. Do your best to stay focused on your final destination, and leave your options open for alternate ways of reaching your target.

The Game: Mental Or Physical?

Golf is both a mental and physical game. To play golf, it is imperative that you develop your physical skills. While performing these skills, your mind directs your body and your body performs perfectly whatever your mind dictates. Your mind's means of directing such performance is the process of imagery. This is a fact of human existence. You create an image with your inner eye, and your body reacts to the image. As long as you trust the natural process, your performance will be good. However, if you doubt the process, then you will get in your own way.

One of your first goals is to learn how to use your inner eye to create these images. Your next goal becomes staying committed to them. *Therefore, the key to performance is in learning how to program the proper images, and then trust your inner eye to direct your body into action.*

The hardest part of the whole process is learning to *let* the images direct your actions. When you let your body react to the images, you feel absorbed in the activity of the game. Listen to the interviews of professional athletes after experiencing extraordinary performance, just about every one of them will say they were "in the zone," the "bubble," or some other state where they simply reacted to the images of the desired actions. However, when athletes perform poorly, they constantly describe a lack of focus. Their minds are full of distractions and interferences. Their images are vague, or hazy at best.

Interference is commonly experienced as any kind of *uncertainty*. Your response to such uncertainty may be fear, tension, or any other form of anxiety. For example, when faced with a difficult shot over trouble, you may be uncertain of how hard, how high, or how far you need to play the shot. That is exactly the point at which you experience *doubt*. If you're going to learn how to play under such pressure, you need to learn how to create crystal-clear images of the shots you desire. Then you simply need to react. In this way, golf is just as much a reaction sport as any other. Sports whose activity capture your attention, and keep your mind fixed on the game, seem to readily create the images for you. When you're captured within the fascination of the game, the powers of your subconscious mind are free to be creative, and responsive, creating the necessary imagery. Try to realize, it's really you who creates the images, and it's you who reacts to the activity of the game.

Think of tennis for example. We call tennis a reaction sport. What is it that you react to? Is it simply the movement of the ball? Or do you also react to the rules of the game? The court has boundaries you have to play within. Do you react to your awareness of where these lines are? Do you also react to the rule that you can only allow the ball to bounce once? Do you react to the rule that you must play the ball over the net? So, as we chase the ball down, we have all these rules and guidelines to react to. We have already created a scenario, or image, in our mind's eye about how we must react.

Baseball is the same. It's the rules that create the scenarios about when and where we throw the ball. When batting, we react as much to the count and the on base situation as we do to the moving ball. We also react to the instructions of the third base coach. That whole process is based on the scenarios of the moment. Which is to say it's based on how you perceive the moment. It's based on what you are aware of in the moment. Golf is once again the same

Great golfers understand the fascination of the game and react to its activity. Though the game of golf has more down time then any other, the activity is ongoing. When you become fascinated with this activity, you find yourself in the zone. While in the zone you find yourself reacting to the images your inner golfer provides. Without being in the zone, you are challenged to create the images for yourself. Whether mesmerized by the ongoing action and suspense of sport, or challenged to create your own fascination with the game, realize that it's your responsibility to create the proper images. Whether consciously aware or subconsciously induced, it is still your responsibility.

The Way We Learn Imagery

So, images are more than just visual pictures. They capture as much of the feel of the experience as they do the picture. When I say feel, I actually mean sensitivity. We commonly like to say that we had a feel for the experience. However, this feel may capture sounds and tastes as much as touch. Therefore, by feel we really mean sensitivity. We mean that we captured all the kinesthetic sensations that were involved in the activity. This is what makes images much more powerful than visualizations. It is also why we can only become aware of the proper images through experience.

So never forget, imagery is the process of capturing the look and feel of the experience, and it can only be learned through the experience itself.

What this all comes to, is that you must find an approach that develops the fundamental images. Additionally, your approach must incorporate a mind-set that will keep you on track with your chosen goals. More specifically, your approach must provide a way for you to develop your physical skills, it must provide a means of focus so that you can apply the skills, and it must provide a mental perspective that will keep you on track.

The Way Of The Golfer is going to guide you through the process. It will show you how to use imagery to perform your skills, and it will show you how to develop the images through focused attention. The key to this whole process will be learning how to focus your attention on the task at hand. A skill that will be valuable in everything you do.

As you focus your attention on what is happening, you'll become aware of what motions work, and which ones fail to work. Through continual awareness, you will develop complete images of the golfing process. Then as these images become internalized, you'll develop confidence in your ability to focus effectively.

Since it is impossible to internalize the fundamental images as quickly as you can intellectually understand them, you may become impatient and demand of yourself that which is unattainable. You may say to yourself, "If I know what I need to do, then I should be able to do it." However, knowing how to do something is much different than knowing what needs to happen. *Therefore, give yourself the time to internalize the feelings captured in each image. Otherwise you will continually change instructors, techniques, equipment, etc., until you decide to see the process to its completion.*

As a part of their training, every world champion athlete performs daily practice routines. Sumo wrestlers, for example, must perform hundreds of leg lifts a day, martial artists perform daily katas, and gymnasts rehearse their routines daily. These daily routines involve inner training as well as physical conditioning. The inner training involves developing the focus necessary to perform well. It involves understanding the process of imagery. And it is an ongoing process.

The Role Of The Coach

You may wonder why I'm concerned with the issue of coaching. My reasons are threefold. First, I believe understanding the process of coaching can help you seek out an adequate coach. Second, if you decide to learn the game without the help of a coach, then you must become your own coach. Third, I believe every prospective coach needs to understand the responsibilities of being a coach.

One of the main responsibilities of coaching is to draw the student's attention to what is happening as they practice and play. The coach guides his students through exercises that are designed to help them become aware of the fundamental skills. To be effective, the coach must learn how to tap into the student's individual needs. While doing so, the coach must help the student realize what actions correlate to what results. The key here being that the student is first aware of what is happening - the actions, then is aware of how those actions produced the results. By doing so on a continual basis, the student eventually learns how to be self-sufficient.

If you are going to perform consistently and confidently, you must become self-sufficient, because during play the responsibility for performance rests solely in your hands. Thus, without a sense of self-sufficiency, you will have a hard time learning how to trust yourself. By learning how to become self-sufficient, you will have the confidence to depend upon yourself when the pressure is on. At which point I believe you'll be able to free yourself from the assistance of a coach. You'll simply coach yourself from that point on.

At some point you will become aware of what works, and you will be able to inspire yourself to perform your best. I sometimes feel that my students look to me for the inspiration. When they are on their own, they often imagine my voice and what I would say to them. They imagine the way I talk and wish they had an audiotape of my voice to listen to. They sometimes give me a call just to hear my voice, as if there is some magical inspiration in the sound.

This reminds me of what artists and writers go through when they have a creative block. They can only create when they are inspired. If they lack the fascination, if they lack inspiration, they are unable create. When they are absorbed in something, they become fascinated and are inspired to create. Golf too, is a creative endeavor. If you want to create the type of game that is inspirational, then you need to find a source of true inspiration.

You must capture the inspiration first. The physical game rarely creates the inspiration. Instead, finding the inspiration creates the type of physical actions that produce results. You must be fascinated with the process from the beginning. If you fail to begin with the inspiration, it's unlikely the outcome will be inspirational. Remember, the inspiration comes first. Lastly, I believe to play the type of game that will be satisfying, you need to find the inspiration yourself. You must find the coach inside you, and you must use this inner coach to inspire yourself throughout every moment of the game. If you can do that, then you will be truly self sufficient, and you will be satisfied with your play.

Awareness & The Way We Learn

Throughout the centuries, man has always been fascinated with the process of human development. The inner understanding this process uncovers shows us that the way we experience the game is as important as the actual information being learned. You can observe this as you watch children practice and play. *Children are always looking and absorbing, looking and absorbing until they absorb enough information that something connects. Then "ah ha," they are aware of how things work.*

Watch little children on the driving range. Notice how they tee up a ball and simply swing away. When they miss, they wipe it out of their mind and say, "give me another." When they connect, they yell, "Wow," and look around for acknowledgment. The fact is, children learn more efficiently than adults. That is because children pay attention to what is happening as they play, where as adults try to control their learning.

Since the best way of learning is by paying attention to what is actually happening, the best way to coach is by helping students become aware of what their attention is on. This is what real coaching is all about. *Whether coaching someone else or coaching yourself, realize how well you learn by paying attention to what is actually happening during your golfing activity.* As my coach always told me, "There's more value in knowing where the club actually is, as compared to knowing where it should be." If you are unaware of where it is, then how can you direct it where you want it to be? Throughout this process, awareness is truly the key to both learning and performance.

To understand this process more thoroughly, you must understand how your faculties of awareness interact. These faculties involve conscious awareness, subconscious awareness, and *"body knowing, "* or body awareness. Conscious awareness involves the activity of the thinking mind, subconscious awareness involves the activity of the imagining mind, and body knowing involves the sensitivity of the body.

You can think of your conscious mind as speaking one language, your body speaking another language, and your subconscious mind being able to speak both languages. The language of your conscious mind is that of analytical thinking and mental pictures, the language of your body is that of sensitivity, and the language of your subconscious mind is that of imagery. *Since imagery is the process of capturing the look and feel of the given activity, the process of imagery blends your conscious desires with your physical actions. That means imagery is an application of the mind-body experience. Therefore, the process of imagery demands the greatest attention with regard to performance.*

Once your subconscious mind blends the mental picture of the task with the matching sensitivity, an image is created. As you pay attention during practice and play, sensory information is sent directly to your subconscious mind through neurological impulses. As your subconscious mind receives that sensitivity, it acquires the specific information necessary to recreate the given actions. However, if you fail to pay attention to what is happening, then you will be unaware of how those actions occur. That is why paying attention to what is actually happening is more important than understanding the theory of what needs to happen.

As you pay attention to your present environment, you learn through experience. The more often you experience the proper actions, the more complete your subconscious image becomes. As your image becomes more complete, your subconscious mind becomes more educated. The more educated your subconscious mind, the greater your level of awareness.

I hope it is clear at this point that it's your subconscious mind that remembers exactly what needs to happen; and the more often your subconscious mind receives the necessary information, the greater your level of recall. This whole process is continual, and at some point your subconscious mind will internalize a crystal-clear image of the desired skill. Once that level of internalization is reached, you become truly aware of how to do it.

The Performance Mode

To understand how the performance mode works, start by observing something you already know how to do. Think about how you would go about tossing a ball into a basket. If we placed a basket twenty-five feet away, and told you we'd give you one hundred dollars for every ball you tossed in the basket, how would you go about tossing? What do you think about? What do you focus on? What do you feel? You probably focus on the basket and how much energy to give the toss. You imagine the ball flying through the air, and into the basket. You feel the ball in your hand, and your palm facing toward the target. Over time, you've learned that the longer your palm stays facing the target, the straighter your toss. You also learned, the longer the length of your follow-through the longer the length of your toss.

As you perform, you stay focused on the image of what needs to happen. You picture the activity and feel the correlating sensations, thus creating a complete image. Then you simply trust your programming, and react. If you remain focused along the way, you perform well. If you become distracted, you'll perform poorly. *Therefore, your primary responsibility with regard to performance is to imagine exactly what it is that you want to happen. Then react to the image.*

Golf Is An Underhanded Game

Golf is an underhanded game, because we must swing the club in an underhanded motion in order to play the ball off the ground. One way of ensuring that your swing will remain underhanded is to play the game from the ground up. Many of you have probably heard that before. But, what does it mean? We are told that it means we play the game with our footwork as the foundation of our swings. I once heard Sam Snead say, "Good players play from the waist up and great players play from the feet up."

This is an important image because underhanded motions happen below the waist, and over handed motions happen above the waist. It is also important because underhanded motions use good weight shift to help generate the strokes power. And good weight shift is generated with good footwork. This is why great golf is played from the feet up. Conversely, if you have too much upper body action, then your swing will attempt to become over handed before it returns through the ball. And, that is largely the cause of swinging over the top.

Every time I hear the term *"over the top,"* I wonder whether the person that said it knows what "the top" is. Some people say they swing over the top of the swing plane. Others say they swing over the top of the ball, and yet others say it is the right arm swinging over the left. So, what exactly is the top, and what is swinging *over the top*. Most golfers would agree that swinging over the top involves a re-routing of the golf club outside during the transition from backswing to downswing. However, most professionals would agree that Sam Snead re-routed to the outside without swinging over the top. The reason Sam Snead's motion was considered valid is because he employed good footwork to drive his weight underneath as his swing moves forward through the ball. What I am saying is that swinging over the top is actually a weight shift problem, instead of a swing path problem.

Let's take a closer look at this process. As you address the ball and start your backswing, it is beneficial to feel your weight rooted solidly beneath your feet. As the swing progresses, your weight then travels along the ground from foot to foot, back and forth, without rising up in the body. If you allow your weight to move upward through your body as you perform your backstroke, it may rise above your center of gravity. Once your weight moves above your center of gravity, it is said to be on top. I hope it is apparent that anything above your center of gravity is in the upper portion of your body, and is therefore considered on top. So, everything above your center of gravity is on top, making your center of gravity "the top."

Once the weight rises up top, it becomes very difficult to return the weight back underneath before moving forward in the swing. If the weight is on top, and the swing moves forward before it moves downward, then the weight has moved over the top instead of under the top. As soon as your weight moves over the top, the only way you can return the club to the ball is to swing abruptly downward, otherwise you will miss the ball completely. *Thus, it is the improper shifting of the weight that causes the common flaw of swinging over the top. The re-routed swing path associated with swinging over the top is actually the reaction to already being over the top.*

The best means you have of preventing the over the top motion is to develop proper weight shift. As you shift your weight back and forth, feel the weight moving across the ground from foot to foot. By keeping your weight on your feet, you can be sure to keep your weight under the top. While everything moves under the top, and through the ball, you experience the power and control you desire. In this way, proper footwork is the vehicle of proper shifting of the weight.

In the short game, the weight generally never gets on top, so you rarely swing over the top. Have you ever heard the saying, "from waist-high to waist-high every professional swings the same"? Although less than absolutely true, there are enough similarities to make the point valid. From waist-high to waist-high the player's weight is shifting under his center of gravity, and the club is swinging in an underneath fashion. Therefore, it is often a good idea to practice these waist-high to waist-high motions as part of your fundamental training. Lastly, as part of the training, you are going to have to learn how to use your weight shift in the proper manner.

Tossing Is Natural

As you begin developing your short game skills, I want you to consider that the basic short game feel can be accomplished by tossing the ball with a golf club. Tossing with the golf club is a good way of imagining your short game play because tossing is an underhanded motion you have already learned throughout your life. You simply need to incorporate your tossing skills into your golfing images.

When you watch tour players preparing to pitch, chip, or putt, you often see them mimic tossing the ball. Many tour players learned how to play these shots by simply tossing balls around a green. For these players, it is the basic feel for tossing that programs the feeling of chipping or pitching the ball through the air. The accomplished player learns how to toss the ball with the club, instead of his arms and hands. *Thus, the outward feel of the toss, and the outward image of tossing, can be used to direct the precision necessary for executing your short game skills.*

Clubface Awareness

As you learn how to toss with the golf club, you must realize that it's the clubface that controls the toss. The clubface directs the toss much as the palm directs tossing with the hand. So, as you toss the ball with the club, you must be able to feel where the clubface is facing, and how the clubface catches the ball. What I am saying is that you must develop clubface awareness. *Developing clubface awareness, and the imagery that goes along with tossing, are the keys to being able to confidently play your golf shots.*

You can establish this awareness by developing a connection between the palm of your dominant hand and the clubface in which the club simply becomes an extension of your dominant hand. Then you can use that connection to create a natural underhanded motion that will naturally play the ball to your chosen target.

Using Your Natural Hand

If you are right-handed, you have a better chance developing clubface awareness by developing unity between your right hand and the clubface. Since the right-handed player has the greatest sensitivity with his right hand, it makes more sense for the player to use his right hand. The common rebuttal to this belief is that, "If you use the right hand, then your right hand will become overpowering, and you will begin hooking the ball." That is only true if you turn over your hand and clubface. But turning over your hand and clubface is unnecessary. You only need to square them through impact. To do that, you need to feel where the clubface is facing. And you have the best chance of feeling where the clubface is facing by using the sensitivity of your dominant hand.

There is a reason your dominant hand is your dominant hand. It has more dexterity than your non-dominant hand. It can acquire greater feel or touch. In short it is more educated and can command greater control than your non-dominant hand. I know that may sound different from traditional instruction. However, I want you to consider that one of the reasons most golfers fail to improve is because traditional instruction falls short of what is most natural and efficient for our golf games. Maybe there is a more natural way to play.

Keep in mind it is the misuse of your right hand that causes you to misplay your shots. Thus it is the way you use the hand that makes the difference. *The fact is if you are naturally right-handed, you are more likely to misuse your left hand than your right hand. Conversely, you're more likely to use your right hand effectively than your left hand.* If you perform everything else the best right-handed, then why play golf from the right-handers side using primarily your left hand? It's often recommended that naturally left-handed players should play from the right-handers side, and naturally right-handed players should play from the left-handers side. That is because it's supposed to be technically easier to create leverage. Unfortunately the concept is flawed. Leverage is created through a chain of events that blends the actions of your body, arm swing, hands action and the club alignments, as compared to just using your hands.

Additionally, leverage is simply a means of multiplying power. You must first produce it. *You produce power through Rotational Force, shifting weight, and utilizing thrust through muscle power.* It's much easier to pivot powerfully and efficiently from the natural side. It's much easier to control the weight drive from the natural side. And it's much easier to apply muscular thrust from the natural side. Therefore, all your natural instincts will be most efficiently used if you learn to develop clubface control with your dominant hand in control.

From Short Game To Long Game

Once the connection between the palm of your hand and your clubface is established, you can begin tossing with the club. Just as you imagined tossing the ball into the basket, you imagine tossing the ball onto the green. We often have players close their eyes and toss, then open their eyes and toss. Often they toss better with their eyes closed. That is because it is sometimes easier to imagine a good toss with your eyes closed. With your eyes closed you must utilize the powers of your inner eye, and your inner eye uses all your senses instead of just your eyes. While using your senses in this manner it makes it much easier to use your imagination. You imagine where the target is, you imagine the ball position, you imagine how the tossing motion will feel, and you imagine how the ball will fly. As you continue to practice with your eyes closed, you will inevitably experience the proper images time and time again. As you continue to experience how proper imagery produces the desired performance, you'll learn to trust in your powers of imagery.

The basic tossing motion can be used for chipping, pitching, and all partial shots up to the half swing. However, once you're ready to travel beyond the short game, your tossing motion must turn into a swinging, or throwing action. This is because there are limitations to how far you can actually toss the ball. Once you reach this limit, you must find means for producing more power. Thus, the stroke's source of control must move from the arm swing to the body motion. When tossing the ball, your body motion merely accommodates your arm swing. That is because your arm swing has sufficient power to create an effortless toss.

Where greater power is needed, you need to get your whole body involved. Therefore, the pivoting action of your body becomes the controlling force. Even though your pivot is the controlling force of the long swing, your arm swing still commands great attention. This is because your arms swing directs the forces of your stroke through the ball to your chosen target. While your body conveys its power to the arms, your arms and hands must precisely direct these forces to your target. Therefore, whether dealing with the intricacies of the short game or the complexities of the long game, your arm swing and its underhanded motion commands a great amount of attention.

Awareness Skills

The question becomes, how do you learn to pay attention to the most important aspects of the game? As you begin to toss, pay attention to what is happening. Ask yourself questions about how the toss feels. At first, the answers may elude you, simply because you've never looked for what's happening before. Most likely you've been more concerned with what you think you should do, and how it will make you look. However, now it's time to become aware, it's time to pay attention. And you draw your attention to the action by asking questions about what is happening.

For example, ask yourself where the palm of your dominant hand is facing as you are tossing. Then you might ask yourself where the ball traveled in relation to where the palm was facing. If the grip is undertaken correctly, the ball will always travel in the direction your palm and clubface are facing. Ask yourself if your attention is on tossing, or if your attention wanders as you toss. If something distracts you, notice what specifically was distracting. Also, try to distinguish the difference between focused attention, black-outs, or specific distractions.

You can ask yourself, on a scale from one to ten, how clear your image was as you practiced tossing. Was the image clear and strong, or did the image pulsate? On a scale from one to ten, how well were you aware of the clubface and the connection between the palm of your hand and the clubface? Ask yourself whether you feel like you're tossing, slapping, slinging, hitting, or any other type of motion.

Once you have your attention on the necessary motions, your main focus switches to the process of imagery. From putting to the full swing, this process is repeated until you acquire proper awareness of each activity. I recommend that you first experience the complete process with a pitching wedge, nine-iron, or eight iron. Stick with one club throughout the whole sequence of transitions, because the experience from one transition to another is taxing enough without confusing the issue by introducing new variables. Once you've successfully completed all the transitions with one particular club, then you can focus your efforts on the next longer club. If you remain patient and follow the recommended approach, you will be greatly rewarded.

The Process Of Imagery

The images you use to direct your performance are what we call outward images. As far as the short game is concerned, it is the outward image of the toss that directs your performance. If you think too much about the backswing, impact, or any other particular part of the motion, then your mind must shift gears in the middle of the stroke. As your mind shifts gears, the stroke hesitates, and the swing becomes broken into two separate motions. Such an inflection in the motion of the stroke is sure to cause timing and consistency problems. Thus, the act of breaking the swing into separate motions ought to be avoided. You may find that the best way to ensure one continuous fluid motion is to focus on some point past the moment of separation. Better yet, if you focus on the end of the swing, you'll be sure to complete the swing's journey in one continuous motion. So focus on your final destination, focus on the outward projection of how you get there, and simply do what you have to do to follow-through with your imagery.

If you can create the proper images, the question becomes whether you're actually programming the proper images when the necessary occasions arise. If you understand the proper actions, and understand the importance of creating the proper images, but fail to take the time to program the proper images at the appropriate time, then you will perform poorly. You must realize that every shot needs to be approached as the *only* shot. This is why professionals play the game one shot at a time, taking the time to program their images properly.

Touring professionals know the game is a continual test in perception, concentration, and awareness. This is because you must continually assess your position in relation to your target, and then decide the best course of action. To play well, you must choose a course of action you're confident you can perform. Then you must follow-through with your choice. The best chance you have of following through with your choice is to focus on it alone. Actually, in the moment, there is only one shot to be played. And in the moment you can only play one shot at a time. Therefore, make a choice you can be committed to, and focus all your attention on the image that satisfies your choice.

Watch Out For Negative Images

The best players know that if they worry about water hazards, out of bounds, sand traps, or any other obstacles provided by golf course architects, their images will be filled with trouble and uncertainty instead of focused attention. Always remember, the golf course architect provides those obstacles in an effort to distract you, and he challenges you to overcome the mental distractions he provides. Accomplished players know they must focus on where they want the ball to go, and how they want the ball to get there. They know negative thoughts only confuse the task at hand, and they're unwilling to let the course architect's deceptions distract them. Once the proper images are programmed, and you're committed to them, all you have to do is react. Throughout that process, it is imperative you stay committed to your images until your swing is completed. You can become distracted at any point along the way, from the moment the swing starts all the way to the end.

Once distracted, you will quite often fail to become refocused and will forget to finish the swing. As a result, you merely hit at the ball, instead of swing *through* the ball toward the given target. The shot becomes misdirected, because the stroke is performed without a focal point beyond the ball itself. Conversely, if you stay committed to the outward image and finish the swing, you will always swing through the ball toward the target. The shot will travel down the intended line of flight, even if contact is off. Consequently, you will find that every time you properly program the image, trust the image, and stay with the image until the motion is completed, you will experience the results you desire.

That whole process depends on committing to the process of imagery. This is why tour players often say, "you must make a decision and stay with it." You must imagine a shot, choose a club, and then stay committed to your choice. At times you may pull off the desired shot without the proper process of imagery, but these shots happen out of chance, and are never consistent. When it happens by chance, you are never satisfied. This is because you are uncertain you can repeat the task. *Therefore, seek out the proper imagery, and stick with the process until you trust in its expression and the way it directs your actions.* If you can do that, you will truly be satisfied with your play.

Staying Within Yourself

It's easier to trust your imagery if you choose a course of action you're confident you can perform. This is what's meant by the saying "stay within yourself." Staying within yourself means choosing shots you are positive you can perform and sometimes that means you will choose and aggressive play. Once you've chosen a shot you are confident you can perform, you can play the shot as aggressively as you like. As a matter of fact, it is much easier to play a shot aggressively when you are certain you can pull it off. Conversely, it's difficult to be aggressive when you are uncertain of your ability to pull the shot off.

Therefore, staying within yourself means imagining a shot you are sure you can perform, and trusting in your ability to program, commit to, and perform the shot.

As soon as you're uncertain of what you will do, you'll be outside your comfort zone, and you'll feel as if you've lost the ability to stay within yourself. Every player ought to know the boundaries of his comfort zone. Again, if you are positive you can perform the shot, you're within your comfort zone, and you have a good chance to stay within yourself. If you are unsure you can perform the shot, then you need to step back and choose a different course of action.

Every time you notice yourself within your comfort zone, monitor how well you perform. Every time you find yourself outside your comfort zone, notice how poorly you perform.

While playing within yourself ask yourself this question: "If that were the worst shot I played all day, would I be happy?" When you fail to stay within yourself, ask the same question. You'll find that every time you stay within yourself you'll answer yes, and most of the time you play outside your comfort zone you'll answer no. *This is the way I recommend you monitor your improvements. You're truly improving as long as your worst performances are improving.*

Once you understand the limits of your comfort zone, stay within them while playing on the golf course. Does this mean you must stay content with your current level of performance? *The goal of practice is to expand the boundaries of your awareness, and therefore your comfort zone. The goal of performance is to apply the skills you already possess, so play within yourself on the course and expand your skills during training.*

At this point we have covered the fundamental philosophy of the *New Horizons Golf Approach*. As you continue your journey along this path, try to be patient. The longer you stick with it, the better a player you will become. In fact, there is nothing in it to prevent you from becoming a scratch golfer. Good luck and stay focused outward.

Chapter Three
Playing The Game

Why Do We Play Games?

      I often ask my students, "Why do you play golf?" The usual answer is, "Because it is fun." Then I ask, "What makes it fun?" I get a variety of answers at that point, because every golfer gets to decide for himself the purpose of playing the game. However, what I really want to know is, "Why did they play golf in the first place? What continues to attract them to the game? My experience has taught me that golfers continue to play because something inspires them to play.

      So, what inspires us to play, and what keeps us coming back? The game can be so frustrating that golfers are continually compelled to quit the game. However, that same golfer will recommit to the journey even as early as the next day. So what makes the game so attractive? What continues to inspire us to play?

      I believe this inspiration comes from inside us. I believe that playing golf is a creative process, a form of art you might say. Like all other games, I believe we play them because we feel something inside us that we want to express outwardly. All athletes have inner desires. They imagine themselves performing these inner desires. The athlete is just as much an artist. An artist captures some inspiration that he feels inside. The artist imagines expressing this inspiration through his art. The golfer does the same.

I believe we play games to get in touch with our inner selves. Throughout our daily activities, we are usually consumed with our work. We are absorbed in doing things that are only important to us because they put food on the table. Most people work without having a passion for their work. Therefore, they seek out a form of artistry in their play. Sure, some people pick other hobbies as a means of self-expression. But, the athlete expresses himself through sport.

I believe this is why people admire others who have a passion for their work. Whatever you do, your work is an art form if you have a passion for it. If your work is an expression of your inner self, then your work is a form of art. Whether farmer, caterer, banker, carpenter, or painter, you can be an artist as long as you capture the inspiration that drives you to create your work. We all know people that make their work an artistic endeavor, and we admire their passion. We admire how they can become totally absorbed in their work. And we admire how they achieve satisfaction with their occupation.

So, I believe the reason we play golf is to express something that we are unable to express in the rest of our life. I believe we play games to awaken the inner self that we keep locked up all day long. In many ways, the inner person that imagined great things as a child has been locked up and hidden from our daily activities. Games provide us the opportunity to open those locked doors, and to allow our inner self to come out and play. When you think about it, it is this inner you that you enjoy being around the most? If you disagree, then I want you to ask yourself one question. "How do you act when nobody else is around?" Are you the same old proper self? Or do you act with freedom? Do you allow your inner child to come out and be a part of what you are doing? We've all been caught in the moment of allowing our inner child to play. Sure we might have been a little embarrassed to be caught in the moment. However, the moments that led up to us being caught were some of the most enjoyable moments of our day.

What most of us fail to realize is that we keep this inner child so locked up that it is dying to get out and play. It is dying to express itself outwardly. I believe this is one of the reasons why most people are so eager for retirement to come along? After we retire, we can once again reach for our dreams. We can play more often, we can express ourselves through our hobbies more often, and we can get in touch with our inner child more often. We honor the grandparents who seem to be living a second childhood.

The fact is many people live their whole lives that way. They're always committed to expressing their inner desires. They're always in touch with their inner self. Sure it takes a lot of commitment. However, it is worth it. So, when you are playing a game, commit to really playing the game. Get in touch with your inner self, and allow your inner self to express yourself freely. Again, "How would you play when you are all alone?"

Anyone who has played golf for their whole life is certain to have gone out and played a round of golf by himself, even if it was for only nine holes. When you played by yourself, did you care if anyone was watching? Did you feel free to try shots that you would ordinarily avoid? Did you allow your inner golfer to get into your play? I'm sure you did all these things. The fact is, we all want to play with such freedom. We all want to be able to express our inner desires.

Analyst, Hoper, Or *Golfer?*

Although we all want to play with the freedom expressed in the last section, how do most golfers go about playing the game? I believe most golfers are either analysts or hopers on the golf course. I also believe they want to be *golfers*. So what makes you an analyst golfer, and what makes someone else the hopeful golfer? Lastly, what type of golfer do you want to be?

The analyst golfer is a problem solver. He wants to analyze what went wrong with every swing. The analyst is unconcerned with playing good golf as he is with describing what goes wrong. The analyst is like the television commentator that rewinds the video of the players swing and dissects it to show us what went wrong or right. However, if the golfer analysis as he swings he gets "Paralysis by analysis."

While the analyst goes about describing what's wrong with the *golfers* play, the hoper realizes that he lacks the knowledge of what to do, and therefore tries this and that in hopes that he will play good golf. The hoper feels like he's tried everything and is only left with the hope that he will one day find his inner game. The hoper believes that the game has much more to offer, but finds little purpose in the game. The hoper knows that the basic goal is to score as low as you can, but goes about playing without finding the type of purpose that inspires good performance.

The golfer knows that the purpose of the game is to express your inner desires. The golfer knows that to express your inner desires you must stay focused on the image of that desire. The golfer is therefore more concerned with focusing in on what he wants out of his play. The analyst is more focused on fixing the faults of his play, and the hoper, well, is just hopeful. So what do you want to do? Do you want to be an analyst? Do you want a video cameraman to follow you around so that you can analyze everything that goes wrong, or do you want to play golf? Do you want to stand up to each shot unsure of what you should focus on? Do you want to address the ball, swing, and hope the shot goes where you want it to, or do you want to play golf?

I believe everyone that likes to play golf wants to be a golfer. I believe they want to have some purpose to their game. Oh, they may be unaware of wanting to find such purpose, however they are instinctively search for it. Though there are many purposes the golfer can choose, I believe the best purpose is one that helps you express your inner desires. I believe this is what playing golf is all about. So if you want to be a real golfer, commit to the purpose of getting in touch with your inner golfer.

The Purpose vs. The Goal

We all know the basic goal of the game. The goal is to score as low as possible. The goal is set by the rules of the game. It is a part of the framework that defines the game. The purpose of the game is a matter of choice, and each golfer chooses it for himself. Whenever I think of the purpose of playing, I am always reminded of a quote by Marcus Aurelius. He said, "Of each particular thing, what is its nature, what purpose does it serve." So what is the nature of golf, and what purpose does it serve for you? As I've expressed, I believe the nature of the game is to express your inner desires through sport. I believe that at its very nature, golf is a creative process. And since it is a creative process, it involves expression, the expression of your inner desires.

So as you play the game, your basic goal is to score as low as you can, while the nature of the game is to express your inner desires. Beyond this, what purpose does the game hold for you? Does the game provide you a vehicle for exercise? Does it provide you a way of meeting new people? Is it simply a way of getting to know your friends better? Is it a way to express your competitive nature? Is it a means of conducting business? Maybe the purpose changes from day-to-day. The question still remains, what purpose does the game serve in your life?

You may wonder why I bring this up. Well, the only way you are going to reach your goals is to satisfy the purpose of doing what you are doing. If you fail to satisfy the purpose, you will fail achieve the desire results. Which means you will fail to achieve your goals. Remember, the purpose is the thing that inspires you to play. It is also the thing that can inspire you to play well.

Whatever secondary purposes you may choose, I want you to realize that the basic purpose of every creative endeavor is to express your inner inspirations. The inspiration that compels you to play is the most basic purpose that needs to be served. If you want to be a golfer, if you want to play golf, then become more concerned with expressing the experiences that inspire you to play in the first place. Stay committed to the purpose of being out there instead of falling prey to the analyst in your thinking mind. When you find yourself caught in the mode of playing hopeful golf, try to create a new inspiration. Become creative with your shots. Take a chance, express your creativity, and learn from the experience. I'm sure you will find that playing creatively will give birth to inspirational experiences.   In other words, find a purpose that inspires you to be a golfer instead of an analyst or a hoper.

Spending Time Purposefully

If you consider all the different purposes we can choose while playing golf, you will find that most of them can be satisfied in between playing your golf shots. Take meeting people for example. Golf is one of the few activities I've encountered were people openly meet and play with people they've never been acquainted with. Golfers will without hesitation walk up to a pro shop as a single and ask for a game. Sure, the golf professional might assess the player's skill, and try to pair him accordingly. However, given the chance, the golfer will simply be joined up with whoever they can join up with. It seems strange that even though golf is an individual's sport, we golfers are so likely to show our social nature.

How about the golfer that uses the golf course as his office? Any business that is being conducted on the golf course surely happens in between shots. What about the golfer that wants to spend a day with nature? He surely absorbs the benefits of nature more between shots than he does during his swing. What about the golfer who uses the game as a way of getting exercise? I'm sure this golfer will opt to carry his clubs, or at least will walk as much as possible in between shots. I used to play with a gentleman in San Diego we called "Smiley." He was in his 70's back then, and in the middle of a hole, he would get this look in his eye, then take off running. He would run a hundred yards or so at a time. Sometimes he'd run all the way to his ball. He truly enjoyed his time in between shots.

One of the special things about golf is that it provides us ample opportunity to satisfy the purposes we choose for the game. A round of golf provides you over four hours of time to satisfy the purposes of the game. Although you satisfy the basic purpose of expressing your inner desires during your swing, you satisfy all other purposes in between swings. The question becomes, how purposeful can you make your golfing experiences? Will you spend your time in between shots sulking, complaining, analyzing, or contemplating the errors of your way, or will you spend that time productively? Will you spend that time satisfying a worthwhile purpose?

The fact is it's the person you are being in between shots that determines how much fun you have with the game. During the swing you are focused on being a golfer. In between swings you accept responsibility for your actions, and you move on. You move on to the task of creating a good golfing experience. You move on to the task of satisfying the purpose you chose for the day. So I want to know who you are being in between shots. Are you acting like a person that enjoys playing golf? Are you acting like a person that enjoys being on the golf course? Or, are you acting like someone that no body wants to be around? The choice is yours. You can be the type of golfer that creates a purposeful round of golf, or you can be the type of golfer that focuses only on the golf shots and how they produce the score on your scorecard.

Who Do You Bring To The Course?

If you are going to play a game with purpose, then you are going have to be a purposeful golfer. This means, the you that shows up at the golf course needs to be purposeful. It's a choice, and it's a commitment.

As you reach the golf course, which *you* is going to show up? Is it the preoccupied you, busy in mental conversations about what's going on in your life? Are you showing up as the analyst or the hoper? Are you showing up as a perfectionist? Is your ego going to show its face today? Will you show up with the same old attitude, with the same old preconceptions about the game? Will you give in to the pressures of the game? How will you react when the going gets tough out there?

With every moment of your round, you must be committed to being purposeful. You must realize the reasons you are out there, and you must commit to expressing the type of golfer you want to be. Like I said before, it's the person you are being in between shots that is going to create an enjoyable round of golf. So, are you showing up to the golf course as a person that wants to satisfy the purpose, or are you showing up as an opinionated, biased, socially conditioned non-golfer? Are you showing up as someone who is willing to commit to the purpose of the game, or are you showing up as someone that has been conditioned to worry about the score? Are you showing up as someone that wishes to play golf, or are you showing up as someone who is worried about how other people will think about your play? Are you showing up as someone who is willing to learn new things and have new experiences, or are you showing up as someone who has a multitude of opinions about the proper way to play golf? Can you play golf free of being the analyst? Can you leave the analyst at home?

As you prepare yourself to play, make it a goal to bring your inner golfer out of its hiding place. Become committed to bringing the *you* that you like being out to play. Imagine playing with your friends. As you play golf, they introduce you to many of their inner personalities. Which one of those personalities do you enjoy playing with? Now, reverse the process. Imagine the many different *yous* that you bring to the golf course. Which inner you do you enjoy being the most? Which one has the most fun playing the game? And what purpose does this inner you care about?

We all have many personalities, and these personalities have different moods and attitudes. You must realize what mind-set each of these personalities brings with it to the golf course. And you ought to realize how each of these mind-sets affect your focus, your performance, and your level of enjoyment, while on the golf course.

The most productive mind-set is one that is free to choose its own purpose for the game. It recognizes your inner desires and sets out to express them. What I am trying to say is that these choices must be truly yours. These choices must be free of social conditioning. The purpose you choose ought to satisfy your inner desires, instead of your parents' or your friends'. I encourage you to choose your purpose with free will. Do it without intellectualizing, reasoning, or deducing. It ought to come from the nature of the inner you. It ought to be chosen because you feel the purpose fulfills something you feel inside. It fulfills the expression of who you want to be.

Showing up as that type of person can be difficult. We are conditioned to be proper, to approach things with social order. We are conditioned to think before we act. We are conditioned to analyze our actions so that we can avoid repeating our mistakes. We are conditioned to the scientific process of dissecting our experience. We are often discouraged to express ourselves openly.

However, golf is a creative process, and the only way you are going to express the type of game that will be purposeful is to show up as a golfer who can freely express the desires he feels inside. You must show up as a golfer who seeks purpose in his play, instead of results.

"I want you to realize that the basic purpose of every creative endeavor is to express your inner inspirations. The inspiration that compels you to play is the most basic purpose that needs to be served. If you want to be a golfer, if you want to play golf, then become more concerned with expressing the experiences that inspire you to play in the first place. Stay committed to the purpose of being out there instead of falling prey to the analyst in your thinking mind."

Chapter Four
Golf Is A Target Sport

Developing The Fundamentals

As we begin this section, notice that the title of part two was developing the fundamental skills. To play the game, to achieve the basic goals while playing, you need some skills. Therefore, the physical side of the game has an important role in the development of your play. Over time the physical skills will become less of an issue, and the inner skills will become more important. Of course, even after you have developed your fundamental skills, you still need to stay in touch with the physical skills. Golf is a game that requires the use of our body, the club, a golf ball, and a golf course. All these things are physical. Thus, you will always need to be aware of the physical aspects of the game.

The way you go about learning these skills now will have a direct influence on how well you perform them later. So choose your physical skills and the way you learn them wisely. The physical skills must satisfy a physical need. That means your physical skills will involve the necessary skills of putting, chipping, pitching, and swinging. Because, all those skills are needed to play golf. So you must find a basic way of playing each of those shots. In this book, I am going to focus more on the fundamental skills needed to play the long game. So I am going to leave putting aside for now. If you enjoy *The Way Of The Golfer*, then you can find the same approach to putting in *New Horizons Golf's Pocket Coach Volume 9 – The Art Of Putting*.

As you engage in the process of learning those skills, remember that your job as your own best coach is to draw your attention to what is happening as you practice and play. Although I am going to provide you with a basic game plan, your first priority is to be aware of what is happening, then you can compare what is happening with the plan we are setting out to achieve. The best way of learning is by using awareness to understand the difference between what is happening and what you want to happen. So do your best to stay committed to being your own best coach.

Golf Is A Target Sport

As you begin developing your fundamentals skills I want you to realize that each skill has, as its goal, delivering the ball to a target. Every shot we play must have a target. It must be target-oriented. Each shot is played out into the playing field with the goal of eventually ending up in the hole. The importance of this point is that the goal of each swing is to deliver the ball to your target. The ball simply gets in the way of the stroke and is sent to the target.

The more you focus on "hitting" the ball, the less concerned you are with playing the ball toward your target, and the less likely the ball will reach the hole in the fewest number of strokes. If you make the ball the most important thing, you will often fail to swing through the ball to your target. You will instead hit at the ball. Eventually all golfers learn that hitting at the ball fails to work.

I believe that the thought of "hitting" distracts us away from our true intentions of playing the ball to the target. I believe that the thought of hitting gets in the way of swinging through to your target. And if it gets in the way of swinging to your target, then it will get in the way of your true goal, playing the shot to the target. Thus, the fundamental swing involves a motion that is target oriented instead of ball bound. It will be "one continuous fluid motion" as Jack Nicklaus says. Thus, the motion of the swing ought to be uninterrupted as it flows through to your target. It should indeed be target oriented.

As we have heard time and time again, the golf ball simply gets in the way of the swing. And the golfer who approaches his swing in that manner is certain to find a natural way of sending the ball to the target. You must trust your inner golfer to coordinate the catching of the ball. So, *one of your jobs is to produce a free flowing, target-oriented golf swing.*

Thus, as you development of your swing, there are three primary concerns. Preparing yourself to swing, the swinging motion, and finishing the motion. Therefore, your swing is a means of moving from your starting position through your target into your finish. The player that finds a way of connecting a good starting position with a good finish is sure to develop a fundamentally sound golf swing.

The swinging motion that connects your starting position to your finish is performed with your whole body. Even with the smaller swings of the short game your whole body gets into the action. Of course, the more power you need, the more your body gets involved, and the less power you need, the more your body simply accommodates the action. Thus, we must use our body to swing the club, and we must direct our actions through to our chosen target.

As we prepare to swing, we position ourselves in such a way that we can swing towards the chosen target, followed by finishing while facing that target. With that image programmed, golf becomes a reaction sport. We simply react to the image of targeting the swing. If you allow your swinging motion to flow freely, if you allow your inner golfer to direct the shot, then your game will become a responsive activity instead of a manipulative one. You will have the sense of letting your shots happen in a very reactive manner.

As you learn to swing reactively, your swing will feel more natural. It will feel so natural that you will be less concerned with perfecting your technique. Instead you'll be more focused on targeting your shots. The freedom you feel with this natural swing will also afford you the opportunity to be more purposeful with your game. You will be less worried about your technique and what might go wrong.

So, as you develop your fundamental skills, always find a way to make them target-oriented. That means you must find a way to stay focused on delivering the swing in a target-oriented manner.

Tossing It Around

As I mentioned earlier, golf is an underhanded game, and tossing is one of the basic underhanded motions we can use in our golfing skills. Since you've already learned how to toss things around throughout your life, the image of tossing can be a great benefit to your golf game.

You can use the image of tossing with your hand to imagine how you will play the basic short game shots. Then once you have the image, all you have to do is to learn how to toss the ball with the golf club instead of your hand.

As you watch touring professionals, you'll see many of them mimic tossing the ball as they try to acquire a feel their short game shots. Sometimes you can even see them do it before putting. Although they're mimicking a tossing motion, it's the type of tossing motion that starts the ball rolling as soon as possible. Sometimes professionals practice this motion with their hand, and sometimes they practice with the club. In either case, they're trying to acquire a feel for the proper motion. It's hardly a coincidence that this is the same procedure many professionals use to program their short game shots.

Even though you may ultimately want to hole your tosses, your primary goal is to advance the ball close enough to make your next shot. *Therefore, the main goal is to make sure you toss the ball the proper distance.* If you advance the ball the proper distance, then you will be more likely to hole your first putt. Also, even if you miss your first putt, you will certainly be close enough to hole your second putt.

As you develop your tossing skills, you can practice tossing balls over mounds and bunkers, practice tossing the ball high with spin and high without spin, practice rolling the ball across long distances as well as short ones, and practice landing the ball on a specific spot from different positions around the green. As students practice these variations of tossing they often ask, "What's the difference between chipping and pitching?"

The books and magazines we read provide a variety of explanations. Some say a chip is the same as a putt, only you use an iron instead of a putter; and a pitch is simply a small swing. Some say chip shots are performed without any wrist action, and pitch shot use the wrists actively. Some say a chip shot rolls farther than it flies, and a pitch shot flies farther than it rolls. Some say chip shots are low running shots, and pitch shots are high flying shots. Though we describe pitch shots as high flying shots that roll less than they fly, we also play pitch-n-run shots which roll farther than they fly. So then, what's the difference between chip shots and pitch-n-run shots? Deciphering all the available theories can be quite confusing. Let's make it easy. Just think of every short game shot as a toss. Simply look at the shot to be played, and decide what type of toss is appropriate.

The main difference between short tosses and long tosses is the feeling of following through. The more you follow-through, the more energy you feel in the toss, and the further you will toss the ball. You'll feel more and more energy as you follow through longer and longer. Therefore, the only real difference between a short toss and a long toss a sense of greater energy.

Whether you use a lot of wrist action or very little, the activity of the wrists simply determines the type of spin being applied to the ball. The greater the activity of your wrists, the greater the amount of backspin applied to the ball. It's generally the case that little spin is desired with shorter tosses, and greater spin is desired with longer tosses. However that is a generalization, because sometimes we need lots of backspin with very short shots and other times we look for forward spin on long running shots.

When practicing around the green shots, keep your tosses as simple as possible. Pick a spot between the edge of the green and the hole. Then imagine tossing the ball on the spot. Once you have a feel for landing the ball on the given spot, imagine the ball rolling to the hole with the proper amount of speed. This whole process is generally called spot chipping, or spot pitching; however I prefer to call it "spot tossing."

As I practice tossing with my hand, I am focusing intently on my target. I'm feeling how much toss is needed. I focus on following-through to my target, and I allow my body to flow with the tossing motions. Lastly, the palm of my hand instinctively faces toward the target as I release the ball.

As I practice tossing towards a hole, I pick a spot on the green where the tossed ball will land. Then I want to feel how much the ball will need to roll to stop at the hole. This particular toss was judged perfectly, stopping on the edge of the hole.

Develop Tossing Awareness

If you're going to adapt your natural tossing ability into a sound short game, you'll need to learn how to toss with a club. To toss with a club, you must hold the club. The act of taking hold of the club is called "gripping the club." Therefore, your hands grip the club, and *the primary goal of the grip is to control the club and monitor the clubface.* As you take hold of the club, do so in such a way that the palm of the dominant hand and the clubface are aligned in the same direction.

You may have had a hard time developing a sound grip in the past. This is generally because instructors are more concerned with how the grip looks instead of whether the grip is functional. Some instructors tell us to hold the club in the fingers, while others tell us to hold the club more in the palm. However, we rarely read about the actual function of the grip, as well as the proper feel.

Develop a grip that feels firm and relaxed. Firm enough to hold the club without any slippage, yet relaxed enough to allow the arms and hands to swing freely. If the undertaking of the grip produces any tension throughout the arms or hands, the swing will lose both power and control. You can develop a firm grip by understanding how you hold anything firmly. For example, pick up a golf ball and hold it in your hand. Squeeze the ball as if you're trying to prevent a small child from taking the ball out of your hand. As you hold the ball firmly, notice in what part of the hand you hold the ball. Do you hold it in the palm of your hand, in the fingers, or in between the palm and the fingers? Loosen your grip for a few seconds, then close your eyes and squeeze the ball again. Keep your eyes closed, and focus on what it feels like to hold the ball firmly in your hand. Once again, notice in which part of the hand the ball is held.

Your next step is to learn how to feel a firm hold of the club. Have a friend hold a club out in front of you. The club should be held slightly above waist high, the shaft ought to be parallel to the ground with the handle pointing straight at you. Your goal is to reach out and take hold of the club firmly. As you take hold of the club, hold it with your right hand only. Adjust your grip so you feel a good hold of the club. Notice how you hold the club better with your thumb running down the left side of the shaft. Notice how your grip feels most firm when your hand is aligned along the side of the shaft. Rotating your hand under or on top of the shaft will produce undue stress on your wrist and forearm.

Notice the relationship between your hand and your forearm. Does it feel more relaxed when your wrist position aligns the forearm and hand in a straight line, or when the wrist bends making an angle between the two? If you still have trouble finding the feel, take hold of the club again, then lean backwards. As you feel the weight of your body pulling on the club, adjust your hand position until your arm and wrist feel relaxed and comfortable. If you feel excessive tension in your arm or wrist, continue adjusting your grip until it feels firm, yet relaxed.

Once the alignments feel natural, comfortable, and firm, you are ready to practice with your other hand. When you begin to take hold with your left hand focus on holding the club firmly. Avoid trying to make your left hand grip look exactly like a mirror image of your right hand grip. Some player's natural grip will have the hands mirror each other, but it's just as common that they are aligned differently. *The only absolute with regard to the alignment of the hands, is that we want the palm of your dominant hand and the clubface to be aligned in the same direction, and your non-dominant hand must work in unison with your dominant hand.*

Even though I suggested holding it first with the

right hand, left-handed players will reverse the process. You always want to take hold of the club with your dominant hand first. It will be a natural reminder that your dominant hand maintains control of the clubface.

Once you understand how each hand independently holds the club, you are ready to blend together the activities of both hands. As I begin coaching students, I spend only a little time getting my students to establish their grips. I've found that if I allow the player to hold the club in whatever way provides the firmest hold, he can learn the proper fundamentals without worrying about his grip. Even though it can be argued that they have yet to establish a perfect grip, their grips evolve into the best possible grip as they learn more about the fundamentals.

Always remember, it's the goal to be achieved that determines how the tool is to be held. The more you learn about the proper motion, the more you feel the need to adjust your grip. It's like learning how to use a hammer. If the hammer is used for hammering, you hold the hammer one way; but if you use it for pulling out a nail, then you hold it another way. Therefore, it's the goal to be achieved that determines how the tool is held. So to develop a perfect grip you need to know exactly how you are going to use the club, and that takes time. Therefore, in the beginning I am looking for my students to simply develop a functional grip.

For example, have you ever seen someone pick up a tool try to figure out how to use it? The person turns the tool around and around until they figure out what the tool is used for, or until someone shows them how to use it. In either case, the person only learns how to hold the tool properly once they understand its fundamental purpose. Once they know the purpose, and how the tool works, they automatically develop a functional grip. So, as you learn more about the subtleties that involve the fundamentals, you will learn more about the utility of your clubs, and more about how to hold them.

As the private lessons continue, my students inevitably begin to notice they're having trouble reaching a certain fundamental goal. As they continue to struggle, I ask them, "Is there any way you can adjust your grip to make it easier to achieve the goal?" The student thinks about it for a few seconds, and then adjusts his or her grip. The student always makes an adjustment that produces a more fundamentally sound grip.

By the time we finish developing all the fundamentals, the student has achieved his or her best grip. Among these fundamental skills is the ability to acquire clubface awareness. Since you need to develop clubface awareness to play the game, you must develop a grip that allows you to be aware of where the clubface is facing. So, if you know you need a firm, relaxed hold of the club, you'll grip the club accordingly. Also, if you know you must maintain clubface awareness, you'll adjust your grip to achieve that goal. As you learn how to direct the clubface, you'll re-adjust your grip further. Finally, this process will continue until each fundamental is understood, learned, and maintained.

Some people argue that it is impossible to develop the proper fundamentals without first developing the proper grip. This may be true, but it's also true that it is impossible develop all the fundamentals at once. It takes time to develop each individual fundamental. Therefore, you can learn the particular aspects of the grip that pertain to each fundamental as you encounter each fundamental. This allows you to develop your grip naturally, and for the correct reasons. So avoid being too preoccupied with developing the perfect grip before you understand the proper fundamentals. Focus on the fundamentals, and then figure the best way to hold the club in order to achieve these goals.

Thus, as you begin to develop your grip, simply

align the palm of the dominant hand with the clubface, while creating as firm and relaxed a hold as possible. Beyond that, I suggest you position your dominant hand below your non-dominant hand, and then blend the activity of both hands together. Finally, you have the freedom to reach these goals in whatever way feels most natural.

Since it is impossible to privately tutor the development of your grip, I'll provide some guidelines or suggestions as to how you can blend the activity of your hands. There are three types of grips that are commonly used to blend the hands together. They are, the overlapping grip, the interlocking grip, or the ten-finger grip.

The ten-finger grip is established by taking hold of the club with the dominant hand below the non-dominant hand. Once you have created a firm hold with each hand individually, you simply slide the hands together. As you slide your hands together, the thumb of the top hand slides under the thumb pad of the bottom hand.

The interlocking grip is the same as the ten-finger grip except the pinky finger of the bottom hand interlocks with - crosses under - the index finger of the top hand. The overlapping grip is also a variation of the basic grip. The only difference being that the pinky finger of the bottom hand overlaps the index finger of the top hand.

The ten-finger grip is the most underrated of grips. It's the most suitable for players with weak arms and hands. That is because holding the club with all ten fingers on the handle makes it easier to hold the club. The ten-finger grip is criticized because it's said to slow down the activity of the hands and clubface. The truth is, having such active hands is unnecessary. If your hands become too active, they'll have a tendency to turn over too quickly. ***The faster the clubface moves from an open to a closed position, the harder it is to time the squaring of the clubface.*** You can provide a square clubface without using such hand activity. You merely need to feel the palm of your dominant hand and clubface swing through the ball square to the target.

The ten-finger grip provides greater support and control, because it helps keep your hands from becoming overly active. But, it allows your hands to be active enough. So, the ten-finger grip is an excellent choice for players with overly active hands, even if the player only uses the ten-finger grip for training purposes. Of course, these are simply the most common grips that are taught. There are others available as well. So feel free to develop your own variations, as long as they allow you to blend the hands together.

One of the variations that my students have found very effective is the reverse overlap grip. The reverse overlap grip is similar to the traditional putting grip. To hold the club this way, start with a ten-finger grip. Then loosen the index finger of your non-dominant hand off the handle. Once you've loosened your index finger, slide your dominant hand up so that it fills the gap you made when you took your index finger off the club. Once you've slid your dominant hand up into position, feel your index finger cover the pinky finger of your dominant hand. You have just completed the overlap. Since this overlap is the exact opposite of the traditional overlapping grip, we call it the reverse overlap grip. This grip allows you to maintain control with your dominant hand while discouraging your non-dominant hand to grip down too hard. If your non- dominant hand grips down too hard, you will crush the pinky finger of your dominant hand. The pain induced will be enough to remind you to relax your non-dominant hand a little.

Some golfers are skeptical when I mention these options. So, I want you to consider that Steve Jones uses a reverse overlap grip, and he's won playing with it. One of those wins being the US Open. Also consider that Art Wall used a ten-finger grip, and he holds the record for hole-in-ones on the PGA Tour. Moe Norman also uses a ten-finger grip, and he is recognized as one of the best ball strikers of all time. I could continue to list many golfers who have come up with fundamentally sound grips that are non-traditional, or you can simply try one and convince yourself that it is all right.

Notice how the palm of my right hand and the clubface are lined up with each other. Both are facing squarely toward my target.

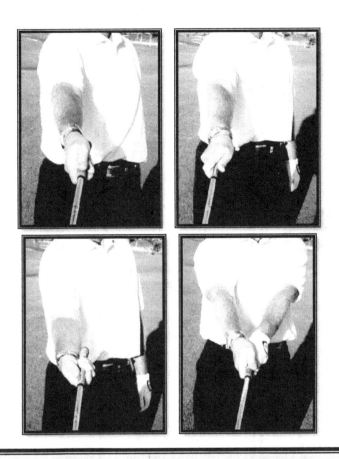

Look at the above photos carefully. In each photo, the clubface was aligned vertically with a square clubface. In the top left photo, the palm of my right hand is aligned square with the clubface. In the next photo to the right, my right hand is rotated on top of the grip creating a weak grip with poor alignment. In the bottom left, my right hand is rotated under the grip creating a strong grip with poor alignment. In bottom far right photo both hands are aligned well with a symmetrical look to the way they grip the club.

(Left) Shows a ten-finger grip. All ten fingers are touching the grip. Unlike a baseball grip where the thumbs hang off to the side, the thumbs are aligned up and down the shaft. (Right) Shows the overlapping grip with the pinky of the right hand overlapping the index finger of the left hand.

(Left) Shows the reverse overlapping grip. The index finger of my left hand overlaps the pinky finger of my right hand. (Right) Shows the interlocking grip. The index finger of the left hand and the pinky finger of the right hand interlock.

Study the photos of the four basic golf grips. All of them are fundamentally sound. As you develop your grip, remember to align the palm of your dominant hand square with the clubface. Then blend your non-dominant hand through one of these methods.

Tossing With The Club

Before you practice tossing the ball, first acquire a feel for the club and the correct tossing motion. Start by taking hold of the club with only your dominant hand. Hold the club firmly with the palm of your hand and clubface facing in the same direction. Then imagine a ball stuck to the clubface. Next, you imagine swinging the club back and forth in such a way that the ball will remain stuck to the clubface. Then on one of your forward swings, imagine tossing the ball off the clubface. More specifically, as you swing the club rearward, imagine the ball remaining stuck to the clubface. Then as you accelerate the clubhead out toward your target, imagine tossing the ball outward. That is the feel you need to toss the ball well.

After acquiring the feel of the tossing motion, you can begin practicing with a ball. When you tossed the ball with your hand, all you focused on was the outward image. You created the outward image by focusing on the target, and figured out how hard you must toss the ball. You then imagined following through toward the target. You will need the same focus as you practice tossing with the golf club.

Let's give it a go! Tee up a few balls, and make a

couple of rehearsal swings imagining the ball being stuck to the clubface. Then imagine tossing the ball outward. Once you have the feel, step up to the first teed up ball, and toss. As you executed the toss, what was your focus on? Did you stay with the image of tossing? Did you focus on hitting the ball? Did you try to scoop the ball in the air? Remember, as you perform the toss, your job is to pay attention to what is happening. Part of what is happening is your focus, and the other part is the physical action.

So, you need to draw your attention to what you are focusing on, and what the physical action feels like. The easiest thing to identify is how the motion felt. Simply ask yourself, was it hitting, slapping, scooping, tossing or some other type of feel. What ever it felt like, it was. You must trust your feel to tell you what happened. As you identify the feel, tell yourself how you liked the feel. Did it feel smooth and effortless? Did they feel like tossing? I'm sure you will find that your tosses feel better than any other option.

Identifying where your focus was may be more difficult to distinguish. However, you need to be able to know where your attention was being directed. You need to know whether your focus was on the task at hand or if your focus shifted gears. When trying to figure out where your focus was, the first question I want you to ask yourself is whether your image is outward or downward. That is, were you 100 percent focused on the outward activity of the toss, or were you focused more downward on hitting the ball?

Sometimes your focus will shift to the ball, sometimes it will shift to swing mechanics, and sometimes it will simply fade away. The fact is, most golfers are unable to focus for extended periods of time. Even staying focused for two seconds can be quite a chore. Throughout your day, your mind flows freely from one thought to the next without need of focused attention. Even as you drive your car, your attention wanders. You'd think you'd need focused attention while driving your car! As you can see, the type of focus you use throughout your daily activities is different than the type of focus you need to play golf. So be patient with yourself, you will learn how to develop focused attention.

Continue practicing your one-handed tosses until you have acquired a clear image of tossing the ball with the clubface. If your arm gets tired practicing with only one hand holding the club, then go ahead and switch to two-handed tossing. However, try to stick with the one-handed tosses long enough to understand how your dominant hand controls the tossing motion.

As you execute tosses with both hands, you follow the same procedure you did with only one hand. The goal is to make the two-handed motion feel as close as possible to the one-handed motion. Using your non-dominant hand will cause you to draw attention to its involvement. As your attention moves toward the addition of the non-dominant hand, your imagery may become more downward than outward. As soon as you lose your outward image, you'll notice you start hitting, slapping and scooping instead of tossing. The result of these ball-bound activities is a loss of control.

The role of the non-dominant hand is to provide additional support to the grip. The non-dominant hand needs to remain very passive through the ball. It merely adds stability to the stroke. If the influence of the second hand is overly distracting, you will be unable to create the proper outward image. When that happens, resume practicing with only one hand until your dominant hand motion becomes completely internalized.

Your dominant hand action must be internalized enough to fend off the urges of the second hand's involvement. Ironically, many students feel more comfortable tossing with only one hand, even after they have acquired the skill of tossing with both hands.

Once you notice your two-handed tosses being executed with your dominant in control and your non-dominant simply going along for the ride, you are ready to apply these skills around the green.

If you continue to find it difficult tossing with two-hands, you can use the following drill. Start by teeing up with two balls side by side. With the first ball, you toss using the one-handed method. As you follow-through, hold the end of your follow-through. After your follow-through has come to a full stop, proceed to take hold of the club with your non-dominant hand as well. In this way, your non-dominant arm and hand can learn to be positioned to work with the natural follow-through of your dominant arm and hand. Notice exactly how your non-dominant arm and hand feel in this position. Then return to the address position while holding the club with both hands. Finally, toss the second ball while focusing on reaching the same follow-through position you developed after making the one-handed toss. After tossing both balls, repeat the process until your two-handed follow-through feels like your one-handed follow-through.

Once you are confidently tossing balls off the tee, you can practice tossing them off the ground. When you first attempt tossing the ball from the ground, you may become a little distracted with the look of the ball sitting on the ground. You may fail to believe that your swing will catch the ball if you simply focus on the image of tossing. You may once again become distracted and focus on scooping the ball into the air, or you may simply hit at the ball. Keep paying attention to the image of tossing, and notice how the clubface tosses the ball when you trust the image. You will eventually be as confident tossing the ball from the ground as you are from the tee. However, if you continue to struggle with tossing the ball from the ground, re-tee some balls until you have your confidence back. Then start lowering the tees until you can confidently toss balls sitting on the ground.

With continued practice, the feeling of tossing with a golf club is the same as tossing with the hand. I actually feel more comfortable tossing with a club than I do my hand.

Playing The Shots

As you practice tossing balls around the green, focus on landing the ball on a given spot, and rolling it to the hole. Watch the ball fly through the air as you toss. Notice whether the ball is floating through the air softly, or darting through the air quickly. Notice whether there's a lot of spin on the ball, or whether the ball has little spin. Also notice whether the ball bounces hard or soft as it lands on the green. Beyond the way the ball flies and lands, watch the way the ball rolls. Doing so will give you valuable insights as to how to plan your greenside play.

Also pay attention to what type of hand action produces a low rolling toss, a high-flying toss, and the standard mid-range toss. *As you toss, you'll notice that the more the palm of your dominant hand faces up, the higher the ball will fly, and the more the palm faces towards the ground, the lower the ball will fly.* Also, notice that the greater the wrist action, the greater the amount of spin. As mentioned earlier, the amount of wrist action simply determines the type of spin that's applied to the ball. If your wrists remain passive, then the ball will tend to float through the air with little spin, and you will find it much easier to control your tossing.

As you continue to acquire a feel for playing a variety of different types of tosses, your main focus becomes that of choosing a particular spot on the green, then tossing the ball so that it lands on the spot and rolls to the hole. In the beginning, you'll simply pick a spot between the pin and the edge of the green closest to you. *As long as you toss the ball on the green between the pin and the edge of the green, you have accomplished your first goal - getting the ball on the green.*

Many beginners attempt tossing the ball too close to the hole. Since they lack the skills to confidently toss the ball to the hole, they become nervous. Once you are nervous, you are likely to chili-dip, chunk, or blade the shot. Therefore, if you're having difficulty getting a majority of your short game shots on the green, simply pick a spot between the pin and the edge of the green, and toss the ball on the spot. If the ball finishes a little too far away from the hole, that's all right. You still have a chance of one-putting, and are almost guaranteed to two-putt.

Once again, focus on landing the ball on the green somewhere between the flagstick and the edge of the green. I like to say, *"land it on the green and roll it toward the hole."* If you continue to watch how far the ball rolls after it lands on the spot, you will eventually acquire the information necessary to accurately play your short game shots next to the hole. It's only through repeated experience that you will learn how to predict exactly how hard and high you need to play your tosses. So continue to practice your spot tossing without worrying about whether the ball will end up next to the hole. In this way you can learn from your experiences.

The right hand is still dominant with my two-handed tosses. My left arm and hand are relaxed. They go along for the ride. The ball once again flies where I am pointing the club in my follow-through.

Extend Your Follow-Through

As you continue to follow through you'll notice the stroke will start feeling larger than a toss. Instead it'll begin to feel more like a swing-toss or a throw. To follow-through longer and longer, you must develop more momentum and release more energy. That means you will follow-through more. To develop added momentum you will naturally swing the club back a little farther. So, be sure to allow the stroke to grow longer.

As you practice these larger motions, you can say to yourself, "swing-toss" or "back-throw." In either case, feel like you are either swing-tossing or throwing the ball. In general, you'll use these motions to play into the green from further distances. Your tosses will be played more immediately around the green where your swing-tosses will be played from further out. As you allow your swings to grow, notice how your body naturally moves with the action. Since you need more energy to play the ball further, you need to allow your body to move more.

As your body moves more freely, notice how you begin to feel your weight rocking back and through with the swing. By letting your weight rock back and through, you are allowing your body to naturally supply energy to the swing. So let your weight rock back and through. It is a natural motion. And you use it all the time when you toss and throw things around.

At this point I'd like to describe what we like to call *Playing Around the Green* and *Playing Into the Green.* Playing Around the Green is what you do when your approach shot misses the green and comes to rest only a few yards from the green. Playing Into the Green is what you do after laying-up out of the rough, or after laying up on a par five, or after misplaying an approach shot some 20 to 75 yards away from the green.

When *Playing Around the Green you will generally use a tossing action* and when *Playing Into the Green you will generally use a swing-tossing action.* These two shots, plus putting, make up your basic short game. Once you've acquired the basic feel for spot tossing, and swing-tossing, you can begin developing confidence in your short game.

In the above photo, you can see that my swing-tossing follow-through is much longer than my tossing follow-through. The key to playing good partial wedge shots is to feel how much follow-through you make. By saying, "swing" in the backswing and "toss" in the follow-through, you can instinctively feel how much follow-through you need to make on your partial wedge shots.

Develop Short Game Confidence

To heighten confidence in your tossing skills, I recommend you develop a specific practice routine. Since the short game is made up of short, medium, and long tosses, as well as short, medium and long swing-tosses, your routine ought to consist of performing each length shot. You determine the length of your shots by controlling the length of your follow-throughs, the longer the follow-through the longer the shot. As you extend the lengths of your follow-through, pay attention to whether you are focusing on hitting the ball harder, or whether you are truly focusing on following through the proper amount.

Your warm-up routine begins by performing one-handed tosses to a short-range target. As you feel confident with your one-handed tossing, you move-on to two-handed tosses. Whether tossing with one hand or two hands, your focus ought to remain on the target and the outward motion of following through.

When you feel comfortable with the short-range tosses, proceed to the medium range tosses, and then to your long tosses. Then you can move-on to your short, medium, and long range swing-tosses.

If you watch professionals warm up for a

tournament, you'll notice they start with a pitching wedge or sand wedge. As the body begins to loosen up, they gradually lengthen their swings. Eventually they work their way up to the full swing.

As you begin your warm-up routine you may find it difficult to acquire a good feel for the toss. If this is the case, it's very likely you're starting too big. So pick a closer target and start with a smaller toss. From day to day, the initial distance will vary. Some days you feel good. On those days, you can start with a target a little farther out. However, on the days you feel under the weather, you'll have to start close, sometimes very close.

In time, your warm-up routine will become the heart of your training program. By executing your warm-up routine on a regular basis it will help you re-enforce your golfing skills. In this way, you are re-establishing your foundation every time you warm up. Additionally, by executing the fundamental skills every time you warm up, you'll maintain a true foundation. This is why your warm-up routine will become the heart of your training program. Therefore, to become an accomplished player establish a sound warm-up routine, and stick with it until the fundamental skills are completely internalized.

In review, practice your one-handed tossing first. Once you have a good feel for one-handed tossing, proceed to two-handed tossing. You will use these skills while playing around the green, and you will apply these skills while spot tossing. As your motions move farther out into the range of playing into the green, you begin practicing your swing-tossing. From here you are ready to travel into the realm of the long game.

Summary Of
The Fundamental Short Game Skills

Our main goal is to keep the short game as natural and simple as possible. To do this you'll incorporate your natural tossing ability into your golf. This means you simply need to learn how to toss with the golf club instead of your hand. Since you toss most efficiently with your dominant hand, *your dominant hand will control tossing with a golf club*. Before you learn how to toss with the club, toss balls around a practice green to get the feel of how high or low you need to toss the ball, as well as a feel for how much roll is needed.

Once you are ready to toss with the club, focus on holding the club with only your dominant hand. As you take hold of the club, align the palm of your dominant hand with that of the clubface. *Once the grip is completed properly, the club will simply be an extension of your dominant hand.* In this way you will be able to simply toss the ball with the club instead of your hand.

Use the *one-handed tossing drill to practice tossing with the club.* Once you feel confident tossing with only your dominant hand holding the club, hold the club with both hands and practice two-handed tossing. If you have trouble with two-handed tossing, use the transition drill to practice first one-handed tossing, and then two-handed tossing.

As you practice tossing with the club, notice how *the ball always travels wherever the palm of your dominant hand is facing.* Practice "spot-tossing" by picking a spot on the green between you and the hole, and focusing on tossing the ball so it lands on the spot. Think, "toss it on the green - roll it toward the hole." As you continue to move further away from the green, you will move out of the *Playing Around the Green* area and into the *Playing Into the Green* area.

To develop confidence in your short game, *stick with your practice routine* until you can feel the difference between short, medium, and long range tosses, as well as short, medium, and long range swing-tosses. Throughout this routine always remember that *the one-handed experience is the foundation of your short game.* Lastly, always stay focused outward on the goal of following through with your tosses. *It is the outward image that will direct heightened performance in your play.*

"You determine the length of your shots by controlling the length of your follow-throughs, the longer the follow-through the longer the shot. As you extend the lengths of your follow-through, pay attention to whether you are focusing on hitting the ball harder, or whether you are truly focusing on following through the proper amount."

Chapter Five
Beyond The Short Game

Beginning With The Finish

As I mentioned earlier, the swing is the motion that connects your set-up to your finish position. The question is, where does your focus begin? Traditionally we begin the quest by undertaking a sound grip and a fundamental address position. I believe we are better off starting with an understanding of how to finish.

Before you can build a sound address position, you must understand what that position is preparing you to do. Of course we know we must play the shot to the target, and to do that we must follow-through to our target and finish off our swing. So, the address position prepares you to swing and finish in a target-oriented manner.

One of the best ways of ensuring your shots will be target-oriented is to make sure your finish is targeted. If you understand how a target-oriented finish looks and feels, then you will find a way to address the ball so that you can swing to the target-oriented finish. This is the main reason I believe we ought to develop our full swing by beginning with the finish.

Let's delve into this process a little more. The finish is the culmination of the swing, and the sum total of the entire swing sequence. Since the finish is the product of the total swing sequence, you can blend together all the fundamentals of the full swing by focusing your attention on finishing properly. In this way the finish is the final destination of the swing, and the beginning of your focal process.

By focusing on the finish, you give your swing purpose beyond merely contacting the ball. As you remain committed to your newly acquired purpose, all the forces of your swing will begin to work together. As these forces work together, the swing's activity will become more synchronized. They will also feel more natural. As you focus on swinging to a target-oriented finish, you will find your shots being targeted as well.

This becomes a powerful aiming tool. Because, as long as you swing to a well targeted finish, you will be targeting your shots well. Once you know this process, you will be able to find your address position more naturally. As a matter of fact, you will instinctually address the ball in what ever way will allow you to finish in a target-oriented manner. This is much like a baseball player does when they are getting ready to throw a ball. The baseball player never thinks about how to stand. He merely prepares himself so he can throw the ball to his target. He prepares himself to follow-through to his target. Therefore, the process of taking up your address position is best served by preparing yourself for how you will follow-through.

Since the finish is the sum total of every moment of the swing, the quality of each individual moment will be expressed in the quality of the finish. If tension exists in the swing, there will be tension in the finish. If the swing is out of balance, the finish will be out of balance. If timing is off, then the body will be misaligned in the finish. However, if the swing is balanced, relaxed, effortless, and well timed, you will finish your swing properly. *Conversely, by focusing on finishing the swing properly you can perform the proper fundamentals naturally. You can perform the fundamentals without dissecting each one individually.*

The Fundamentals & The Finish

If we are going to have a fundamentally sound finish, then we must understand the fundamentals we are trying to achieve in the finish. Remember earlier that I described the finish as completing the body motions. Therefore, we need to understand what body motions are fundamental to a good golf swing. So, by finishing off the basic body motions, we will establish the basic finish.

There are two basic body motions in the golf swing. They are rotating the body, and shifting the weight. The combined effort of these actions is called the pivot. So, the fundamental concern with regard to completing the body motions is that of pivoting to the finish. If all the forces of the pivot are directed to the target, then all parts of the body will finish aligned toward the target. Also, if you are going to transfer all your weight through the ball and out to your target, then all your weight must reach the forward foot by the end of the finish. Thus the basic finishing action is that of shifting your weight completely onto your forward foot, while at the same time completing your body's turn so that you are facing your target squarely.

Now that we understand the basic finish position, let's complete the process by understanding what other qualities make a good golf swing. We all want our swings to be in balance, we want them to be relaxed, and we want them to be as effortless as possible. I believe the key feeling here is effortlessness, because if you want your swing to feel effortless, then all parts of your body must be well balanced and relaxed. *Thus, the proper finish is well balanced, effortless, and relaxed. The body stands tall and natural. All the weight is on your forward foot, and your body is aligned directly toward the target.*

I recommend you spend considerable time learning how to produce the proper finish. Since the finish is a static position, it can be worked on and developed quite easily. Keep in mind, without this foundation, your swing will have little purpose beyond contacting the ball. As a result you will fail to complete your swing, and will never transfer your energy to the target. So, *finishing the swing is an absolute fundamental.* To the beginner it's the most important full swing fundamental, and to the advanced player it's the foundation of his long game. Therefore, you would be wise to train your finish on a regular basis.

Developing The Finish

Since a good finish faces the target, you can begin to develop a good finish by simply standing and facing a target. You can practice this anywhere. Wherever you are, stand up and pick a target. Focus directly at your target and face it as squarely as possible. How do you know whether you're facing it squarely? By paying attention to a couple of checkpoints, you can notice how squarely your finish is aimed. First of all, notice where your stomach is facing. Is it facing directly at the target? Also, notice your chest, is it facing directly at your target? Lastly, are your thighs facing square to the target and are your feet at most shoulder width apart.

Now that you have a feeling of facing the target squarely, check your balance and how relaxed you are. Are you standing tall and relaxed? Are you standing with good posture or are you slouching? At this point, you'll almost feel like you are standing at attention – like a soldier does when they are ready to salute an officer. By this I mean, you are physically aligned to the target and your focus is intently on target as well. One of the common denominators in the finishes of all professional golfers is that they look like they are staring their target right in the face.

As you stand facing the target, your next move is to kick your right foot rearward so as to balance the foot on the toe of your shoe. As the right foot is balanced on the toes, check the alignment of the sole of the foot. We want the sole aligned straight up and down, and facing directly away from the target. Next, check your weight distribution. Is all your weight on your left foot? Are you standing straight up on your left leg? The best way to check your weight distribution is by simply picking your right foot off the ground and standing only on your left leg and foot.

As you pick your right foot off the ground, notice whether you simply lifted the foot off the ground, or whether you needed to push off with the right foot. If you pushed off, you did so because you had too much weight on the right foot. *If you are left-handed, reverse this process. Throughout the rest of this book, please excuse the use of right-handed descriptions only. If you are left-handed, this will require that you visualize the process in reverse. So, I will try to note when this is most necessary.*

Now that you are standing tall and relaxed, facing your target, with all your weight on your forward foot, you are ready to complete your finish. Simply bring your hands together as if you are holding a club comfortably in front of you. Your arms and shoulders ought to be relaxed, and the club will be leaning slightly forward as if it was aligned at your target. You have just completed your finish.

One of the best ways of training your finish is to perform the process in front of a mirror. By doing it in front of a mirror, you can acquire good feedback as to how the proper finish feels once you see yourself in the proper finish. Therefore, the mirror will give you feedback as to how a good finish looks, and at the same time you will understand how your finish feels when it looks proper.

You may notice that your left foot is pointing at the target at this point. That's all right. As you continue developing your skills, I will give you drills that will help you find the proper alignment of your forward foot. For now I just want you to feel what the basic target-oriented finish feels like.

As you settle into this finish position you may notice you have trouble maintaining balance. This is because you are unaccustomed to standing only on your left leg. It is unlikely that you do anything on a daily basis that requires you to stand on one leg and face a target. Therefore, if you want to develop enough strength and balance to do so, you will have to train your finish position on a regular basis.

On the next couple of pages you will be able to view photos of the basic finish position and a drill that can be used to train that finish position. Use those photos and a mirror at hope to train your finish on a regular basis. Once you've mastered your basic finish position you will be ready to learn how to swing to your finish. I will cover both swinging to and turning to the finish in upcoming chapters.

Notice how I am facing the target throughout this whole drill. In the second photo I kick my right foot rearward, placing all my weight on my left foot. Then I take hold of the club and point it at my target. Lastly, I check my balance by lifting my right foot off the ground. Learning to stand on your forward leg will help you develop greater balance in your finish and throughout your swing. Although I am beginning this drill by holding the club in my left hand, I advise that you hold the club in your right hand. That will promote dominant -hand control throughout your whole routine. The more often you hold the club in your dominant hand, the more likely you will maintain dominant hand control throughout all your golf activities.

Once again, I begin by facing my target. Then I kick my right foot rearward while placing all my weight on my left foot. I then take hold of the club and point it at the target. Lastly, I check my balance and weight distribution by lifting my right foot off the ground and balancing on my forward leg. Notice how my posture is tall and relaxed throughout the whole process.

Journeying To The Finish

Once you have the feel for your basic finish, your next goal is to learn how to travel to the finish. Before we do this, I'd like to restate the fundamentals of the full finish. They are: *1) your stomach faces the target, 2) all your weight is balanced on your forward foot, 3) your arms and shoulders are as relaxed as possible, 4) and your posture is tall and well balanced.* With this restated, we're now ready to embark on our journey to the finish.

Since the basic body motion is the pivot, we will begin this journey by learning how pivot to our finish. As with every other part of the game, we are more concerned with the outward actions that deliver our shots to the target. Therefore, when working on our pivot, we will be more concerned with the forward motion of pivoting into our finish position.

The basic pivot drill involves the motion of pivoting around the left side with all the weight on the left foot. To practice this motion, all you have to do is to stand tall and relaxed with your feet a comfortable distance apart and your weight evenly distributed. You then place your hands on your hips and shift your weight over to your left foot. At this point, all your weight needs to be on your left side, your hands need to be on your hips, and your left hip and shoulder need to be over your left foot. Finally, all you have to do is to rotate around your left leg until your knees touch and your hips face a target 90 degrees from where they started. Then you simply return to the starting position and repeat the drill. *Left-handers, reverse the process.*

Although the pivot action combines the rotation of the shoulders and hips, the center of the pivoting action needs to be in the hip girdle. If the hips pivot, the shoulders will follow effortlessly. On the other hand, the shoulders can rotate quite generously without the hips adding anything to the pivot action.

As a side note, if you pivot from the hips, you will extend your chain of leverage from the clubhead through your hands, arms, shoulders, and into your hips. Whereas, rotating from the shoulders will only extend this chain of leverage from the clubhead to the shoulders. Though the latter may be sufficient for the mid to short irons, it is insufficient when greater power is needed with the long irons and woods. Thus, if you are going to develop a good amount of power in your swing, you are going to have to learn how to pivot with your hips.

It's extremely important you keep your hands on the your hips as you perform the pivot drill. If you place your arms across your shoulders, you'll tend to draw attention to your shoulders, and will therefore rotate from your shoulders. Conversely, if you position your hands on your hips, you draw attention to your hips, and will pivot from your hips.

As you execute the pivot drill you may find it difficult to rotate your hips 90 degrees from where they started. If you find it impossible to rotate them 90 degrees, then you will have a hard time rotating them so that your stomach can face the target. The issue here is conditioning. If you lack the flexibility to rotate your hips 90 degrees from where they started, then you need to acquire greater flexibility. You may also need to acquire greater strength. With your left foot anchored in the address position, and your hip rotating around the pillar of your left leg, your leg is going to torque. Since it is unlikely you torque your leg this way on a daily basis, you are going to need to condition your leg to the activity of pivoting to your finish.

By executing the pivot drill on a regular basis you will develop this conditioning. With daily training it will only take a few weeks for you to condition your left leg to the task of supporting a full pivot. Treat this conditioning like working out in the gym. Only pivot as far as you comfortably can. Then when you reach the limit of your flexibility, apply a little more pivot to create a little extra stretch. Just like with any type of stretching, stretch slowly and comfortably. With regular conditioning, you will develop greater rotary flexibility, and you will develop it without getting hurt.

Interestingly enough, most golfers that hurt their lower backs do so because the muscles of their legs and hips lack the flexibility needed to pivot in the manner I am describing. So, by performing your pivot drill on a regular basis, you will help condition your body in such a way that will help prevent any lower back injuries.

To start the Pivot Drill, place your hands on your hips, then shift your weight onto your forward foot. Next, rotate around your forward leg in as tall and relaxed a manner as possible.

Develop A Centered Swing

Even though the issue of where you rotate from is largely an issue of technique, there are some fundamental concerns that make the activity of pivoting from hips an essential issue. These concerns include, 1) the ability to be truly centered about your body's best balance point, 2) the ability to remain as relaxed as possible while completing the pivot, and 3) the ability to maintain proper timing throughout the swing. These three issues are linked to the activity of maintaining a centered pivot. Also, the combined efforts of these activities produce the effortlessness necessary to play enjoyable golf.

With regard to centeredness, your true center of gravity is located a few inches below your navel. Physiologically this is your breathing center, and, it's also your awareness center. Since your physical center, your breathing center, and your awareness center are all located in the same area, there is strong evidence to support the fact that rotating about this center is a fundamental issue.

The more centered your pivot remains about a single turning point, the faster you can rotate. This can be exhibited quite easily by observing the activity of swinging a ball on the end of a string. As you swing the ball around and around, you'll notice you can accelerate the rate of rotation quite easily when you focus about a single point of rotation. As the circular motion of your hand becomes more and more centered, the speed at which the ball swings around and around becomes greater. You may also observe this activity at the end of an ice-skating routine. As an ice-skater finishes his routine, he begins to spin around and around. He starts the rotary activity with his arms and hands extended out away from his body. As he continues to finish the routine, he pulls his arms and hands closer to his body. As the arms and hands move closer to his body, they're moving closer to his center. The result of this is an extremely fast and effortless rotary activity.

It's also important to add that the more balanced your rotation, the faster you can rotate, and a sure way of maintaining good balance is to make sure your rotation is as centered as possible. This whole system of having a centered and balanced rotation is the key to creating an efficient transfer of energy. If you utilize these same principles, you will find yourself enjoying a smooth, efficient, and effortless motion.

The ability to remain as relaxed as possible throughout the entire pivoting motion is also dependent upon remaining as centered as possible. If you are going to remain as relaxed as possible, then you must breathe properly. To breathe properly, you must sustain as deep and continuous a breathing pattern as possible. You will find that the center of proper breathing is located at the very bottom of your abdomen. You can locate this breathing center by taking a deep breath, then exhaling all the way out. As you continue to inhale deeply and exhale completely, your breathing pattern will become deeper and deeper. As the inhaling becomes deeper and deeper, the exhaling will become extremely settled. Eventually, your exhaling will completely bottom out. At the moment the exhaling bottoms out, you will feel completely settled. It's at this settled point that you will find the exact center of your breathing.

It's from this point that your deepest breath both begins and ends. To maintain proper breathing you must rotate without disturbing the pattern of your breath. During this experience, you feel like you maintain a calm, relaxed, centered breath. It's as if you are gently holding your breath in the palm of your hand, while everything outside the center moves around in a circular manner. Physically, this is exactly what needs to happen. If the body is to remain as relaxed as possible, the mechanical motions of the body must work as efficiently and effortlessly as possible. Therefore, by centering your rotation about your center of gravity, you can facilitate both relaxation and effortlessness.

The point at which you become totally settled is also the point at which you will find your awareness center, and it's from the awareness center that your body is directed into action. When we say we experience something, where do we experience it? When we have a gut feeling, where do we experience the feeling? When we experience a physical instinct, where do we experience the instinct? When we say we know how to do something, where is it that we experience this knowing? Even though we gather conceptual knowledge in our mind, we gather awareness in our body. This is what is meant by the term "Body Knowing."

Once you've acquired this "Body Knowing" your subconscious mind uses the understanding to program the desired actions in the future. The subconscious mind does this by transforming the information obtained through awareness into images. As you create the proper images you send your body the necessary neurological responses to direct your body's activity. Your body simply reacts to the images created by your subconscious mind. Thus, the power of your subconscious mind, and your ability to become truly aware, command great attention.

So, your journey to mastery must follow the path of proper breathing, and that path both begins and ends at the very center of your being. To maintain balance, relaxation, and centeredness, your external actions must always move symmetrically around that center. And to tap into the experience of "Body Knowing," you must tune into your awareness center. All these activities happen around a central place, the place that your actions come from.

Pivoting & Finishing

Once you know how to pivot to the finish, your next goal is to learn how to attach the arm swing to the pivot. The Pivot Drill involves rotating the body to its finish position while shifting the weight over to the left side. However, pivoting to the finish is only part of the actual swinging motion. We must also learn how to follow-through with the arm swing. This involves connecting the arm swing to the pivot. Since the completed swing involves synchronizing these actions, we must find some way of blending the arm swing into the pivot.

This being the case, your next drill will be the Pivot-N-Finish drill. The Pivot-N-Finish Drill will focus on connecting your arm swing to your pivot in a way that blends these activities into one continuous motion. Finally, even though connecting your arm swing is a large part of the Pivot-N-Finish Drill, the main goal of the drill is to learn how to finish your swing properly.

The activity of swinging to the finish must be well synchronized, and the motion of your swing must move directly to your finish. If your swing fails to travel directly to the finish, you must compensate. Therefore, the goal of finishing the swing is to both end up in the proper finish and to swing as directly as possible to the proper finish.

While playing, we must finish each and every swing we make. And I believe it is impossible to overstress that point. I know from my own experience that it's only the things I've taken to their completion that I am happy with. In contrast, I tend to be very unsatisfied with anything I've ever left undone. In golf, you must make your choices and stay committed to them until the job is done. By focusing on finishing, you can practice this goal-achieving process. At the same time, you will develop the skills necessary for playing sound golf.

To perform the Pivot-N-Finish Drill, you begin the same way you began the Pivot Drill. Pick a target, 90 degrees from where you are facing. Stand tall and relaxed with your weight evenly distributed, and your feet a comfortable distance apart. Then you take hold of a club with your normal grip. As you hold the club you allow your arms to hang down with your hands and club centered in front of you. As your arms hang down in a relaxed manner, hold the club with the shaft parallel to the ground, pointing straight away from you. That's the starting position. Next, shift your weight over to the left side. Then pivot around the left side, just as you did with the pivot drill.

When your stomach faces the target, your club will be pointed at the target. Avoid moving your arms independent of your body as you pivot. Maintain the connection between your body and arms. I only want the arms to move when the body moves them. *Lefthanders reverse this process.*

As you begin this drill, I want you to feel your elbows contacting your body near your hipbones. If you look in a mirror from the front view and draw a line straight down the center of your body, you can imagine this centerline as an axis of symmetry from the front view. As you execute the Pivot-N-Finish Drill, always attempt to keep your arms centered on this axis.

Symmetry is extremely important when it comes to connection through the ball. As a matter of fact, once the swing begins to release its stored energy, it will continue to release this energy outward until the swing reaches this centerline. It's at this point that your arm swing reaches the full extension. So, it's at the full extension that your swing has completed releasing its energy outward.

From the full extension to the end of the follow-through, your swinging motion is absorbing the left over momentum of the swing. Thus, your follow-through acts as a means of recoil. Furthermore, the longer your arms maintain their connection, the straighter and more consistently you will play your shots. Therefore, it's extremely important to focus on these connection points as you practice the Pivot-N-Finish Drill.

Some people may argue that the elbows never actually stay connected to the body during the swing, and therefore maintaining these connection points will fail to simulate a real swing. Even though this may be true, it's the alignment between your elbows and hips that's important. Even if the arms move slightly away from the body, we still want them to maintain their connected alignments. Therefore, the connection is less a physical lock as it is a spacial relationship between the elbows and hips. By becoming aware of how this connected relationship feels, you will strive to maintain it during the critical parts of the swing. So this drill will establish a feeling of your arms being connected to your pivot as you continue to pivot to your finish.

Now that you've completed your pivot and are aligned toward the target, proceed to hinge your arms over your left shoulder. Avoid lifting your arms up and over the shoulder. Instead, feel much more like you're hinging your arms, at the elbows, up and over. As you swing, your arms will be carried upward by the momentum of the swing. If you intentionally lift your arms and hands over the shoulder, you will most likely do so during the actual swing. As the momentum of the swing acts upon this lifting motion, your arms will raise too high. As your arms swing too high, they'll cut off your ability to breathe properly, thus producing tension, and robbing your swing of power. So, while performing the Pivot-N-Finish Drill, simply hinge your arms up over the shoulder. Then allow your arms to return in front of your body. As your arms return to a centered relaxed position, you have reached the actual finish. Finally, you reconnect your elbows to their initial contact points, and repeat the drill.

Throughout the Pivot-n-Finish Drill, maintain a tall and relaxed posture. Focus on your arms and club moving in sync with the body. As I pivot from the photo on the far left to the one next to it, notice how my arms stay centered in front of my body. In the third photo I complete a full follow-through over my left shoulder before returning to my final finish position. As my body pivots, the arms simply remain connected. I only move my arms up and over the shoulder once my pivot has stopped. Practicing in this manner reminds me that I want my pivot to control the swing instead of my arms.

I recommend you execute both the Pivot Drill and the Pivot-N-Finish drills 50 to 100 times a day every day. Keep in mind that these drills are as much conditioning drills as they are a way of helping you develop a good swing technique. By performing these drills regularly, you will both internalize and maintain the proper pivoting and finishing skills. As you execute these drills, pay attention to what you are doing. If you want to get the most out of these drills, then you will need to pay attention to how you perform the drills. Avoid simply going through the motions. Pay attention to how centered your pivot feels, pay attention to how connected your arms feel, pay attention to how relaxed and balanced you feel. Compare your feelings to the image of what you want to perform. If you have trouble visualizing these motions, or if you are unsure how your motions look, then return to doing some mirror work. Doing the drill in front of the mirror will give you valuable visual feedback that can be matched with your feelings to create crystal clear images of what you want to do.

Understand The Lateral Shift

At this point some people bring up a concern with regard to shifting over the left side. Some people might argue that such a shift is a sway. Not so. A sway occurs when your weight or body moves laterally outside the foundation of your stance. This can be seen when your knees or hips move beyond the vertical boundary of your stance. Picture your legs and stance creating a pedestal for you to pivot around. If your legs maintain their basic A-frame shape, they'll resist the coiling of the upper body, thus creating a platform from which to generate and unleash power. If your knees give way, they'll lose the capability to resist the coiling action, and the pedestal will break down. At that point the shifting of the weight drives the knees outside the base of your stance. Consequently, your hips will tend to slide, losing their centeredness.

Thus, a sway is a breaking down of the pedestal with a lateral motion. This pedestal loses its resistance capabilities only when your lower body moves outside the base of the stance, so a slight lateral motion within the base is acceptable. Also, establishing this pedestal is a concern of the basic fundamentals, whereas precisely centering up your rotation around this pedestal is a matter of fine-tuning.

Secondly, although your swing will stay centered as you move through the ball to the full extension, the swing's center may move slightly forward as the swing progresses throughout the follow-through. This experience of moving "up and out" in the follow-through helps absorb the left over momentum of the swing. Therefore, the "up and out" motion helps establish a recoil, and recoil absorbs the left over energy of the swing.

The Swinging Motion

Now that you understand how to create the basic pivot, it's time to develop the basic swinging motion. First, establish your finish position by performing the Pivot-N-Finish Drill. Once positioned properly, you hinge your arms over your shoulder to the end of the follow-through. From this position, you simply swing directly backward to the top of the backswing, and then directly back to the finish. Repeat this process three times. While swinging back and forth, strive to feel the stroke as one continuous motion. At first the drill might feel awkward. This is because starting from the finish position is a new process. Keep in mind, the purpose of this drill is to develop the basic swinging motion, and the main focus of the swinging motion is to swing to the finish. Thus, continue to practice this activity until you've developed the proper swinging motion.

It's also extremely beneficial to incorporate this drill into your rehearsal swing and pre-shot routine. The purpose of the rehearsal swing is to program the proper sensitivity of the swing. Before you perform the swing, you create a mental picture of what you want to do, then you perform a couple of practice swings to acquire the exact feelings that correlate to the chosen picture. Once you experience a good rehearsal swing, you are ready to swing directly to the finish.

In the past, you've always programmed your swings by setting up and thinking "back-hit." By this, I mean you focused on making a technically good backswing, followed by an effort to "hit" the ball properly. Therefore, whenever you start your practice swings from your conditioned address position, you are likely to program an image of "back-hit." However, if you start your rehearsal swings from the finish, you will instinctively become more focused outward, and you will become more concerned with swinging to your target and finishing your swing. As you address the ball with the intent of playing a shot, you will perform better if you remind yourself to finish your swing, "Finish, finish, finish, swing to your finish." Constantly remind yourself how important it is to finish your swings. You can also remind yourself to follow-through to your target. Follow-through to my target and finish it off, follow-through to my target and finish it off, follow-through to my target and finish it off. Constantly remind yourself of these goals. Then as you swing, pay attention to whether you are achieving those goals.

As you practice starting from you finish and swinging back and through, we call this drill the Swing-Back Swing-Thru Drill. You can use the saying as a kind of song to dance along with. Even as you play your shots you can say to yourself, "Swing-Back Swing-Thru." By saying the song in your rehearsal swings, you will internalize the idea that your goal is to swing back and through to your finish. Then as you set-up to the ball, the song will remind you of those goals. It's a good way of anchoring this image into your pre-shot programming.

During the Swing-Back Swing-Thru Drill, I start in my finish, and end in my finish. My goal is to feel a free flowing, rhythmic swing in both directions. As I swing I focus on maintaining good posture and good balance, and I am focused on finishing my swing aimed directly at my target. I avoid thinking of this position or that position in the Swing-Back Swing-Thru Drill. My goal is to feel a unified rhythmic motion from start to finish without any thought of achieving a mechanical swing. When I can swing without interruption from start to finish, I know I am swinging well.

So, be more concerned with feeling a pure swing than you are making a mechanically perfect swing. I'm sure you find that the more unified the swing feels as one rhythmic action the better your swing will be. And I assure you, the better the swing, the better your shots, and the more enjoyment you will get out of playing this crazy game.

(Next Page) Is a photo sequence that shows the Swing-Back Swing-Thru drill in full sequence. Notice how I start from the finish position and swing directly back to a full backswing. Then I swing through to my finish in one fluid, continuous motion.

Turning On The Power

It's your ability to rotate back and through to the finish that generates the energy necessary to play the shots of the long game. As the body generates this energy, it swings the arms into motion. Once in motion, the body will continue to impart its stored energy to the arms until the body stops rotating. If the body is going to control the arms through separation and into the finish, then the body must finish its rotary activity. The Swing-Back Swing-Thru motion has sufficient energy to play your normal shots with your sand wedge, pitching wedge, 9 iron, 8 iron, and 7 iron. Once you begin to practice with a 6 iron or 5 iron, you'll begin to feel like the Swing-Back Swing-Thru motion is insufficient in the power department. I like to think of it as being more inappropriate. This is because, although the Swing-Back Swing-Thru motion has sufficient energy to play good shots with the longer irons, most players are unhappy with the distance they might achieve. Therefore, as you begin to practice with the longer irons, you'll need to channel additional power through the swing.

As you search for additional power you must look to the activity of the body, focusing on the quality of your rotation as well as the quality of your weight transfer. We'll focus first on rotational force, because it will produce additional power more efficiently. To create greater rotational force, all you have to do is to think "Turn-Back Turn-Thru." Thinking turn-thru instead of swing-thru will place more emphasis on the efforts of the body. With a more aggressive turn to the finish, you'll deliver greater rotary power through the swing. Thus, you'll produce the additional power necessary for the longer irons. The transition between *swinging* to the finish and *turning* to the finish may occur between the 6 iron and 5 iron, or between some other clubs. However, it's definitely the case that you will swing more to the finish with the shorter clubs and turn more to the finish with the longer clubs.

Weaker players may find the need to turn to the finish with a 9 iron or 8 iron. Stronger players may find they begin turning to the finish at the 4 iron. The most accomplished player will be able to either turn to the finish or swing to the finish with any club. For these players, it's simply a choice of which motion is more appropriate for the given conditions.

The Turn-Back Turn-Thru method is performed by turning your hips fully and freely in the backswing, then completing the forward motion by turning your hips through to the finish. As the hips turn to the finish, they will lead the arms and hands throughout the downswing and follow-through. I've found that the thought, "hips first - hands follow" helps many players stay focused on the proper timing between the body and the arms. This timing allows you to guarantee that your hips will control the turning motion through to the finish.

When you are swinging back and swinging through, your body initiates the swinging motion in such a way as to deliver the arms to the finish. In essence, the body motion is throwing the arms through the follow-through and into the finish. As this throwing action occurs, the awareness you feel in your hands controls the release of your swing's energy as you follow through to your target. When you focus on turning through to the finish, your hips compel the arm swing through separation, the follow-through, and into the finish. Thus, it feels much more like the body is carrying the arms through to the finish. This also means it feels like the body controls the release of the swing's energy while turning to the finish.

For the body to control the arms throughout the forward motion, the arms must be connected to the body. As we discussed with the Pivot-N-Finish Drill, we establish this connected relationship by feeling the alignment between the player's elbows and hips. More specifically, it's the relationship between your right elbow and right hip that's most critical.

In the Turn-Back Turn-Thru motion, you'll feel as if your right elbow is connected somewhere near the seam running down the right side of your pants. As you begin to turn your hips toward the target, you'll feel the right elbow return to your right side. Once the right arm is connected to the right side it simply feels like the right hip carries the right forearm and club through separation, into the follow-through, and the finish.

Earlier I mentioned the feeling of connection being that of maintaining the relationship between the elbows and the hipbones. Now I've mentioned connection being the relationship between the right elbow and the seam running down the right side of the pants. Technically, you can connect the right arm anywhere between these two points. If the right elbow tries to move forward of the hipbone, or stays too far behind the seam of the pants, the timing of the swing will be off. Thus, proper delivery of the swing's energy will be impossible. So why would we choose one connection point over another?

The further back we connect the elbow, the longer the chain of leverage, and the greater the power output. Since we need to generate more power with the longer clubs, it's desirable to create a longer chain of leverage. Therefore, it's more appropriate to feel the connection between the elbow and seam line. Even though this is the case, you must make the final choice of what connection points you will use. And that choice will ultimately involve the way your body is built and what swing technique works best for your needs. *Left-handers, reverse this process.*

The Turn-Back Turn-Thru Drill is similar to the Swing-Back Swing-Thru Drill. You start from your finish and end in your finish. Only this time you focus on making a more complete turn in both directions. Notice my full turn at the top of my backswing. Then notice how far I turn-thru on my follow-through. My right side is much closer to the target than my left side, a sure sign I turned through fully. On the next page there is a swing sequence of the full Turn-Back Turn-Thru drill. If you compare that swing sequence to the one of swinging back and swinging through, you will notice that a turn much more fully in both directions.

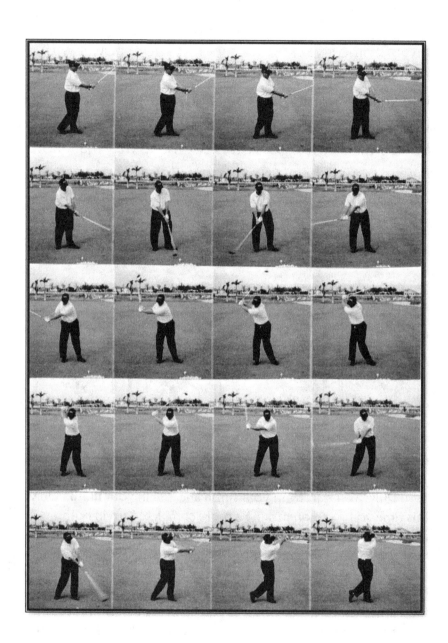

Setting It All In Motion

    This may seem like an unusual time to discuss the beginning of the activity. However, now that you understand how you want to finish and how you move through to the finish, you can position yourself for the task. The whole focus of the address position is that of preparing yourself for the activity of playing the shot. As you take up your address, you must establish a sound foundation. By this I mean you must establish a platform from which you can unleash the swing's stored energy. The way you establish this platform determines how you must start the swing into motion. For example, if you are tense at address, then it'll be difficult to start the swing smoothly. As a result, you will tend to jerk the swing into motion. *Therefore, undertake the address position in a way that let's you swing freely and naturally.* This means the body ought to be as comfortable and relaxed as possible as you establish the swing's platform.

    You establish this platform by building what we call the pedestal - the support system of the golf swing. You build the pedestal by positioning the legs to support a stable center of gravity. If your legs are positioned too far apart, your body will be unable to rotate freely. If your legs are too close together, your center will become unstable. Therefore, while creating the pedestal, your legs need to be positioned to facilitate a stable center of gravity while your body rotates freely.

You can imagine this pedestal as an A-frame support structure. The base of the A-frame runs along the ground from the inside of one foot to the inside of the other foot. The sides of the A-frame run up the legs along the inner thighs toward your center of gravity. As the inside muscles of the legs create a firm foundation, they must do so without creating tension. To further stabilize the pedestal, your weight must settle downward onto the feet. *You can only achieve this sense by living into it. You must feel your weight, and let it settle.* I'll offer one hint. Focus on your breath, and feel how everything tends to settle as your breath becomes deeper and more relaxed. As your breath settles, your center will settle, and you will begin to feel truly grounded. Once this position is established, you are ready to start the swing in motion.

To practice your pedestal, locate a mirror, stand in front of it and assume your address position. Notice how wide your stance feels. Also notice whether your legs feel more underneath your center of gravity, or do they feel wide enough apart that your center is unsupported by your legs? Your legs need to be underneath you enough to create a pedestal for your center of gravity to sit upon.

Once you feel your legs supporting your center of gravity, imagine grounding your weight on your feet. Imagine someone handing you a sand bag. If you had to hold a sand bag while in your address position, how would you stand? Where would your weight be? How much flex would you feel in your knees?

Now that you have this feeling, hold your arms out to your side. Position your elbows at waist-high, and your arms will be even with the seam lines in your shirt. From here, rotate your hips back and through as you try to maintain the pedestal. It will be impossible to rotate back and through fully, and it will be impossible to shift your weight completely in both directions. Instead you will feel like you are twisting your weight into the ground. As you rotate back and through your arms need to work in unison with your hips. Remember, the goal of this drill is to understand how to establish a good pedestal with your legs under your center of gravity. Then as you pivot back and forth, you must maintain the pedestal.

Once you start swinging, you must also be sure you maintain the integrity of the pedestal. The support you feel in the inside of the legs will help limit lateral movement. If there's too much lateral movement, you will feel it in the knees as well as in your center. So, whether swinging to the finish or turning to the finish, one of your chief concerns is that of sustaining a sound pedestal. Without it, you will be unable to accurately and powerfully transfer your energy to the target.

Once you understand the pedestal drill, go back to the Swing-Back Swing-Thru Drill and practice swinging to the finish while maintaining the pedestal. Then follow up your practice by doing the same with the Turn-Back Turn-Thru Drill. You simply need to incorporate the importance of maintaining the integrity of the pedestal.

On the next page you can view photos of the pedestal drill. During the Pedestal Drill I am focusing on supporting my center of gravity. As I maintain my center, I focus on turning back and through in as centered a manner as possible. I can feel my weight twisting across my feet, and my arms feel like they stay symmetrically in plane with my torso. Notice how my arms are in line with the seam line in my shirt in both photo 2 and photo 3 from the left.

Summary Of
The Fundamental Long Game Skills

      To journey into the long game, you must find a means of producing additional power. This means you must look to the efforts of your body. While utilizing the potential of the body, you must bring all the fundamentals together. We do this by starting with the finish. Remember, *the finish is the sum total of every moment of the swing, and the quality of the finish will express the quality of the entire swing.*

      The proper finish is well balanced, effortless, and relaxed. The body stands tall and natural. All your weight is on your forward foot, and your body is aligned directly toward the target. *This final position is the product of a well-executed pivot, weight transfer, and arm swing.*

To develop the finish, use the Finish Drill. Then to learn how to move to the finish, use the Pivot Drill and the Pivot-N-Finish Drill. Once you've conditioned your body to perform the necessary skills, you are ready to develop your actual swing. That means it's time for you to practice the Swing-Back Swing-Thru Drill. As you continue this journey through the long game, you are ready to turn on the power. When ready, turn your efforts to the Turn-Back Turn-Thru Drill. Then you'll prepare yourself to set these swings in motion by practicing the Pedestal Drill. Along the way, stay committed to your outward imagery and the quality of your outward motions. *Lastly, remember it's the activity of the body that determines the quality of your finish, and it is the activity of your arms and hands that determines the quality of your follow-through.* So follow-through with your play to direct your shots, and finish of your swings to make sure you project sufficient energy.

Chapter Six:
Fine Tuning Your Skills

Finding The Source

The point at which you find your center of gravity is also the point at which you'll find your awareness center, and it's from this center of awareness that you commonly experience your gut feelings. If you've ever heard the phrases, "Always trust your first instinct," or "Never second-guess yourself," and believed them to be true, then you'll enjoy the importance of finding your awareness center. Remember the discussion earlier on the languages of the subconscious mind, conscious mind, and sensitivity? Do you remember the term "Body Knowing?" When you experience gut feelings, you are tuning into your sense of awareness. By finding your awareness center you can come to understand what is meant by having the mind and body become *One*. As you experience this sense of oneness, you are sure to understand the true meaning of "Body Knowing".

Within this experience, you find the type of clarity of mind and body which brings you totally present to your environment. At that point, you know for yourself the experience is totally pure of heart. For the individual there's nothing more true than the experience itself.

So, consider that we have these gut feelings because we truly sense the event is going to happen. Also consider, we may acquire these gut feelings because we've experienced exactly what needs to happen. In either case, we have gut feelings because we are aware of a connection between our selves and the present environment.

With this in mind, it's my opinion that these experiences are more than merely coincidence. For myself, I know it's a fact that our gut feelings provide a gateway to the inner realms of the game. They are an expression of our mind-body connection, and they reveal awareness between ourselves and the outer world. If you're still skeptical, then just think of the sheer number of times your gut feelings have actually proven to be true. Then ask yourself, could they all be coincidence?

One of the keys to performance is allowing yourself to trust in your instincts without conscious analysis. If you over-analyze these instincts before you act on them, you'll disrupt the instinctual image. In that case, you'll miss the opportunity to tap into the powers of the inner game. This is the reason people say, "he who hesitates, loses." For if you hesitate even for a split second, then you've lost the opportunity to completely let go and trust yourself. On the other hand, if you experience a gut feeling and immediately act upon it, things usually work out. It's generally the people who doubt themselves, or question their instincts, who have the greatest trouble with performance. Those who learn how to be courageous, and take the chance of letting go of their doubts, will follow the instructions provided by their gut feelings. With such freedom, you can truly learn how to play extraordinary golf.

For many readers this all sounds nice, but how do we apply it in our practice? By focusing on breathing exercises, you'll notice you become completely settled at the moment you allow your breath to totally leave your body. Notice I said, "as soon as you *allow* your breath to totally leave your body." By this I mean, avoid trying to blow all the air out of your body. In an effort to blow the air out of your body, you'll most likely hold some of your breath back. You must let the air leave your body as you do at the end of the day when you settle into the couch and allow yourself to simply say, "Ah, it's all over." As you say, "Ahhhhhhh," and completely melt into the couch, you truly let all your breath leave your body. Once your breath becomes extremely settled, you experience a moment of true clarity. Within this experience everything is all right, the mind becomes totally quiet, and the body is completely relaxed. You feel a moment of complete joy, and all the worries of the day have been lifted from your shoulders. At this moment, the mind and body become *One*.

You can think of your breath as a journey to and from this moment in time. As you inhale you prepare yourself for this moment of clarity. As you exhale, you take the journey back to your center. When the breath reaches its final resting point, you experience this ordinary, yet elusive, meeting of mind and body. As quickly as you found this center of relaxation, you begin the journey back to what we call the real world. If you try to hold on to this place, you'll find yourself merely holding your breath. The more you grasp to hold on to your settled point, the more likely you will only hold your breath. Although every breath provides us with the opportunity to find this most settled of places, most players only take the journey part way to the center of their breathing. In either case the journey is always there to be taken. You can think of it as a tool. A tool that's always ready to be utilized. It's simply waiting to be found.

The key to being able to utilize this tool is in understanding the path of proper breathing. If you learn how to breathe properly, then you'll begin to understand the powers you have locked up inside yourself. Therefore, to assist you in finding the path of proper breathing, we're going to introduce what I consider one of the best golfing drills. As well as helping you experience the path to proper breathing, this drill will assist you in the fine-tuning of your physical swing. That is because, in order for you to breathe properly, every component of your swing must work in perfect geometric alignment with every other component. By simply paying attention to the quality of your breathing, you can learn exactly what must happen for your body to remain perfectly centered and relaxed. As you perform in this way, you are certain to develop the proper synchronization and geometric alignment of every component of the swing.

The breathing drill I'm talking of is called the *Awe-ing Drill*. To perform the drill you simply take up your stance and begin exhaling while saying *"awe."* Even though *Awe-ing* sounds funny, stick with it. It's one of the two best drills for fine-tuning your golfing skills. Although it's generally used as a fine-tuning drill, the beginner can use it to assist in the development of the proper fundamentals. As you practice your awe-ing, you would be wise to focus only on the quality of the *"awe"* and ignore considerations of technique. This is because, if your awe-ing is perfect, then your swing will be the most suitable swing for your physiology. Therefore, your best awe-ing swing will technically be your best swing.

As mentioned earlier, the Awe-ing drill is one of the two best drills you can use to fine-tune your physical skills. The other part of this duo is training with your eyes closed. To do that, you must further focus on the centeredness of the activity. That is because maintaining balance while your eyes are closed requires you to locate your center of gravity. This may sound easy, however, most people go throughout the day with an inherent fix on the visual horizon. It's that unconscious fix that enables you to maintain balance within the visual world. Once the visual fix is taken away from you, your sense of balance within your environment is altered. With the visual fix eliminated, you must maintain balance by sustaining a stable center of gravity.

Training with your eyes closed will both heighten your sense of balance and help you begin to take the journey inward. Since it is impossible to depend upon what you see as you play with your eyes closed, you must learn how to trust your imagery and the powers of your subconscious mind. If you begin to make conscious calculations with your eyes closed, you are certain to lose trust in your skills and begin to second-guess your awareness. Thus, you must trust your inner senses.

Furthermore, as you train with your eyes closed, you must use all your other senses to become aware of your actions as well as your environment. A good way of training with your eyes closed is to try to guess where the ball is going before you open your eyes and take a look. You may need an assistant to help you with this drill, or you can trust your own instincts.

As you train with your eyes closed, ask yourself, "Where's the ball going?" Once you've finished the swing and guessed where the ball is going, open your eyes and see if you can visually pick up the flight of the ball. The more you pay attention to the feel of your swing and the outward projection of your energy, the more you'll be able to actually know the true flight of the ball.

If you have a hard time picking up the flight of the ball when you open your eyes, find a friend who can assist you. As you train with your eyes closed, have your assistant watch the flight of the ball. Once you've guessed where the ball is going have your assistant confirm how close you were to predicting the ball's line of flight. At first it will feel like a prediction. However, over time you'll become aware of the ball's actual flight.

Having a sense of where the ball is going before you actually look for it in·flight is critical to your ability to target your shots accurately. As you feel the direction of the ball's flight, you will also feel what motions correlate to that type of flight. Over time, you will acquire a feel for the subtleties of your swing. By understanding how these subtleties affect the direction of your shots, you are sure to understand how to program these shots when the appropriate time arises.

Whether you use the eyes closed drill to develop a heightened sense of balance, to become more aware of how to target shots, or to acquire a greater feel for the workings of the inner golfer, the eyes closed drill is certain to help you fine-tune your golfing skills. With this in mind, you can use this drill while putting, tossing, swing-tossing, or any other length swing up to the full swing. Finally, once you feel you have developed a feel for the basic motions, I recommend you spend much of your training time using awe-ing and eyes closed drills to fine- tune your play.

"The breathing drill I'm talking of is called the Awe-ing Drill. To perform the drill you simply take up your stance and begin exhaling while saying "awe." Even though Awe-ing sounds funny, stick with it. It's one of the two best drills for fine-tuning your golfing skills. Although it's generally used as a fine-tuning drill, the beginner can use it to assist in the development of the proper fundamentals."

Chapter Seven
Maintaining Your Skills

The Warm-Up Routine

Now that you understand all the basic motions from tossing all the way through turning to the finish, you'll focus our attention on developing a complete training routine. This routine will be used for practice during the development stages of your learning, for warm-up before you play, and for maintenance on an ongoing basis. As you perform this routine, there are a couple of things you need to keep in mind. *(1) The routine involves executing each type of motion from the basic toss to the full swing. That means you must understand the differences between each motion as the swing progresses from the smallest of motions up to the biggest ones. (2) Secondly, the routine also involves practicing those qualities that are the same among all swinging motions.* By understanding how every length motion is simply a variation of every other length motion, you can understand the differences without making the system too complex. Also, by understanding that every motion must maintain the same qualities, such as rhythm and timing, you will understand how your whole routine brings all the shots of your game into one cohesive system of play.

As you now know, the basic progression of shots starts with tossing the ball, then swing-tossing, followed by swinging to the finish, and ending with turning to the finish. As you perform the warm-up routine, keep in mind that the shots you use are divided into four main areas of play.

These shots are, *(1) playing around the green in the short game, (2) playing into the green in the short game, (3) approaching the green in the long game, (4) and positioning the ball off the tee in the long game.* Playing around the green is generally a matter of tossing, playing into the green involves swing-tossing, approaching the green is a matter of swinging to the finish, and playing the ball off the tee involves turning to the finish. *Whatever length motion you're practicing, certain qualities must be maintained. (1) You must stay focused outward, (2) You must feel the outward motion, (3) You must follow-through with the necessary amount of energy, and (4) The outward motion must be played in as efficient a manner as possible.* On the upcoming pages I have described each part of this routine so that you can use it as a reference guide when you need it:

One-Handed Tossing

As you begin tossing, feel the palm of your dominant hand and clubface working together. Remember, the golf club is simply an extension of the hand. Imagine the ball being stuck to the sweet-spot of the clubface. Then imagine tossing the ball out into the range. Next, practice tossing the ball off the ground. If you feel more comfortable, you can practice tossing the ball off a tee instead of the ground. Imagine the ball, the sweet-spot, and the target all belonging to the same activity; and it's the motion of the toss which connects them all together. *As you practice tossing, feel the motion, focus on how much energy is needed, and pay attention to how long-n-smooth your follow-through feels.*

Two-Handed Tossing

A sound two-handed toss will feel much like the one-handed toss. As you toss with two hands, notice whether your dominant hand is in control of the toss, or whether your non-dominant hand is trying to take over. I recommend right-handers toss with the right hand in control, and left-handers with the left hand.

The non-dominant hand just goes along for the ride. When you have trouble with two-handed tossing use the transition drill to toss one ball with a one-handed motion and then a second ball with a two-handed motion. By transitioning back and forth, you will be able to develop the same feel with both methods. Begin with the short-range toss, followed by medium-range tosses, then long-range tosses.

Swing-Tossing

The swing toss feels as it sounds. You swing the club back, then toss your energy outward. The dominant arm and hand still control the motion as the non-dominant side goes along for the ride. While swing-tossing, the body begins to add energy to the tossing motion. However, the body's main function is to accommodate the motion. As with tossing, you commit to practicing short, medium, and long-range shots. *As you continue the routine, your follow-through must remain long and smooth as you follow through with the proper amount of energy.* Finally, when you've played your longest swing-tosses, you have completed the around-the-green and into-the-green portions of the warm-up routine.

Short Game Warm-Up Routine

With every motion of the short game, the arm swing commands the greatest attention. Though the energy for these shots comes from the shifting weight and minimal body pivot, it's the job of the arm swing to convey the energy of the swing to the target. If your arm swing fails to follow through with the proper amount of energy, then the shot will fail to reach the target. As the shots of the short game grow from tossing to the swing-tossing, the activity of the body must accommodate the arm swing more and more. *Once again, your arms and hands add much touch into these shots and therefore the arm swing can be said to have tremendous influence on the quality of these shots. And one of the main focal points of the arm swing is that of following through long and smooth with the proper amount of energy.* Once your short game warm-up is completed, proceed to the long game practice.

Finishing The Swing

As you journey into the long game, you must locate an additional source of energy. To do that we look to the body and its ability to produce rotational force to produce more energy. To harness your body's power, focus on completing a full rotation of the body, while transferring your weight toward the target. Remember, it's your body motion that finishes the swing, while your arm swing simply follows through. Use the Pivot Drill, and the Pivot-N-Finish Drill, to program a proper finish.

Swinging To The Finish

Establish your finish position, then rehearse swinging back and through three times. Next, set-up to a ball and rehearse swinging to the finish. While swinging to your finish, keep your focus on your target and imagining the shot.

As you finish your swing properly your stomach will be facing the target, your weight is on the forward foot, and your body is standing tall and relaxed with good posture. As with every other shot, the motion feels long and smooth with the proper amount of energy following through to the target. As you swing to your finish, your arms follow-through up and over your shoulder, then they'll recoil back in front of you into a relaxed position, your hips will face the target, all your weight will balance on the forward foot, and you will be standing tall and relaxed with good posture. *Whatever length follow-through is applied, always finish tall and relaxed with your body facing the target.* Avoid trying to hold the end of the follow-through. To do so, you would have to conserve energy to hold your arms up at the end of the follow-through. Any energy conserved to hold your arms up at the end of the follow-through is energy we held back from being transferred through the swing to the target.

Up to this point, the long game warm-up will have been completed with a short iron. Once you have warmed up to a full finish with a short iron, you can start working your way up through your set. You may pick an eight iron or a seven iron next, whichever you feel you can comfortably proceed with.

Turning to the Finish

As you progress from the short irons, to the middle irons, to the long irons, you'll notice the need to generate greater energy through the swing. At some point you'll notice that swinging to the finish fails to transfer enough energy to keep you happy with the distance you're getting. In general, you'll be happy with swinging to the finish up to about a 7 iron or 6 iron. However, once the warm-up has reached the 5 iron, you'll notice a definite need to generate more energy. Weaker players may experience this need somewhere around the 8 iron, or 7 iron. To generate greater energy focus on turning to the finish. Turning to the finish demands you utilize the potential of your body to generate more energy. To do that focus on the Turn-back Turn-Thru Drill, and then apply it while playing shots.

Fine-Tuning Your Skills

Once you've finished your warm-up routine, you can use the Awe-ing and Eyes Closed Drills to fine-tune your focus. Awe-ing will help you relax your mind and body. It will also help you develop better rhythm and timing. Your Eyes Closed training will get you in tune with all your senses. It will help you become aware of how to stay more centered. It will help you trust your powers of imagery, and it will help you find the courage to play through mental distractions. Lastly it will help you learn to be truly aware of the flight of your shots.

Summary of The Warm-Up Routine

Once you've completed your warm-up routine, you're ready to go out and play. *Throughout the whole process of warming up and playing, remember to stay outward, feel the proper amount of energy, and follow-through long and smooth.* Remember that the goals of the warm-up routine are to internalize and maintain the proper golfing skills as well as to prepare yourself to go out and play.

The body, the mind, and the mind-body connection must be exercised on a daily basis if they're going to be conditioned to play. To exercise this connection, you can practice "awe-ing" while you swing, or practice with your eyes closed while you swing. You can perform these drills with any one of the motions used in the warm-up routine. Whether tossing or swinging to the full finish, both "awe-ing" and eyes closed training will help fine-tune the mind-body connection. Before playing, prepare yourself by reminding yourself of the proper skills. Use the warm-up routine as a vehicle to being prepared.

Finally, once you've mastered your warm-up routine, you are ready to test your acquired skills out on the golf course.

As you prepare to play, remember to have fun with the game. The golf course is the test and it's going to provide many challenges. If you forget to have fun, your game will become work instead of play. Therefore, focus on playing with your skills, instead of working at them.

"By understanding how every length motion is simply a variation of every other length motion, you can understand the differences without making the system too complex. Also, by understanding that every motion must maintain the same qualities, such as rhythm and timing, you will understand how your whole routine brings all the shots of your game into one cohesive system of play."

Chapter Eight
Know Your Inner Golfer

Letting Your Inner Golfer Play

Up until now we've been discussing what I call the outer boundaries of the inner game. This is because, as long as we're discussing the workings of the mind in conjunction with the body, we are still maintaining our connection to the outer realms of the game. To this point, all efforts to cultivate our game involve a matter of conditioning the mind and body for the task of playing. *From this point on, we must learn how to use awareness to direct our performance. Therefore, the goal of playing becomes much more an inner journey than an outer one.*

Although the results of our play will have definite links to the outer world, everything we do up until the moment of action is controlled by the inner golfer. Even so, it's impossible to escape our link to the outer world. Let's face it, the playing field is built out of the environment, and therefore, by definition it's a major part of the outer game. However, the actual mechanism that sets the whole process of playing in motion is distinctly inner.

So what do we mean by letting the inner golfer play? As far as performance is concerned, it's the subconscious mind that directs our performance.

Thus, the inner golfer is the subconscious golfer. When I stated earlier that the mind directs the body, and the body performs whatever the mind tells it to, I really meant the subconscious mind. Although the conscious mind can become aware of our actions, think rationally, and make decisions, it is unable tell the body what to do. It can try, it may think it's in control, but the body never listens to it. This is the root of the saying, "paralysis by analysis." When the conscious mind is constantly trying to tell the body what to do, it creates distractions that get in the way of our inner programming.

If you think about all the actions you make on a daily basis, you think very little about how to do them. You merely focus on what you want done and do it. Through continual experience you become aware of the proper motions. Once you acquire this awareness, you simply trust your abilities. Once you decide to take action, all thought is put aside, you simply do it. If you stop to think, you get in the way of yourself and make mistakes.

Awareness provides us with all the information necessary to take action. The way we use this information is by first assessing the present environmental conditions, then making decisions based on our present goals. Once we've made an educated decision, and have chosen a course of action, we turn over the task of performance to our inner golfer. *The way we do that is by programming the image of what needs to happen. Then we simply react. In this way, golf is just as much a reaction sport as any other. Therefore, the key to performance is to program a crystal-clear image of what you want to do then let your inner golfer play.*

So your inner golfer is the creative you. Your inner golfer is the one that imagines what you are going to do next. The inner golfer is the inner you that creates and expresses your inner desires. Thus, your inner golfer is the you that desires so strongly to show the world what you can do. This being the case, when you allow your inner golfer to play, you fulfill your inner desires.

Although this all sounds nice, how do you put it all into practice? The first step is recognizing the experience as it happens. For it's only through experience that you can truly understand how this process works. You may ask, "How am I going to experience it if I don't know how to do it?" The fact is, it happens all the time. You simply fail to recognize it. Everyone lets their inner golfer play on occasion. It might only be once a round, but everyone lets it happen. All you have to do is to look for the experience. Pay attention until you recognize it happening. Then you will know what it's like to let your inner golfer play.

It's often the case that you experience the inner golfer play as you're putting. When you're standing behind the ball the image of the line simply appears in your mind's eye. Then you acquire a feel for the ball rolling into the hole. Next, you feel exactly how much energy it takes to roll the ball into the hole. For some reason you get a real strong feeling that this is exactly what needs to happen. It all happens within a few brief moments. However, within those few moments you create such a strong sense of awareness that you know in your gut the putt is going in the hole. For you, you are absolutely certain that something extraordinary has happened. You know all conscious manipulation was eliminated, and you know something special has just occurred with your game. Though you may think these occurrences are extraordinary, they're within continual reach, and they're closer to ordinary than supernatural. As a matter of fact, on those days when you perform extraordinarily well, you are simply performing shots that are within your present capabilities. You simply perform them extremely well. This is the meaning of extraordinary: to perform ordinary skills extremely well. Since these experiences are truly within your reach, you simply need to learn how to tap into them.

Think about your presence when those special shots occur. Sometimes it's on a chip or pitch, sometimes it's on an approach to the green, and sometimes it's on a drive. Whatever the shot, you'll notice you simply imagined the shot with your inner eye and reacted. If you performed the shot without the proper image, then you know for yourself it was just lucky. With your best shots, all conscious thought is eliminated, so are doubts and uncertainties. There's simply a strong image of what needs to happen, and a response that goes with it. This is the essence of letting the inner golfer play.

To let your inner golfer play, you must learn how to let go of your fears and doubts. You have to stand up to the shot and take a chance. As you begin to take the chance, you may ask, "what if?" I'm asked all the time, "How do you stop caring about what happens? How do you stop worrying about the score?" First of all, you need to realize that the score is simply a result. And results simply happen. They follow the actions that produced them.

If you're worried about the score then you'll always be creating negative distractions. It's your approach to the game that really matters. If you approach the game consistently, then your performance will grow consistent. If you're happy with your approach, then you'll be happy with your play. However, if you think too much about the score, then you'll continually feel like you're riding the roller coaster of golf.

Think about those times when you have the feeling you're going to play a good shot. You stand up to the ball and stripe the shot straight toward the flagstick. As the ball leaves the clubface, and is flying toward the pin, you feel elated with joy that you've done exactly what you knew you were going to do. In that moment, you're truly happy with your play. In the next split second, you realize the ball is going to fly over the green and into the rough. At that point, some players get mad and call it a bad shot. Players who react that way are generally focused too intently on the score. They've lost focus on the process. They only care about how many strokes it takes to get there. They can skull the ball to within two feet and still be happy.

As some players watch the good shot flying over the green they say, "Oh well, it was a good shot anyway. Too good." The player who brushes it off that way does so because he's more concerned with the quality of his swings and play than he is with the score.

He knows that over time, good swings will produce better scores. He takes the good with the bad because he knows that even though he just experienced a so-called bad break, his next shot may render him a good one. With this type of attitude, the second player is free to take a chance. He feels free to let go of his doubts, because he knows that doubts are certain to create poor play. He also knows that it's much more fun to take chances and go with the flow than it is to be afraid of every step you take.

As you learn to take a more carefree attitude to the game, you're certain to become too carefree. That's alright. Many great players go through this transition. As you begin letting go, it's difficult to focus your energy toward a given target. You simply let it go out there, anywhere. As time goes on, you'll learn how to direct your energy toward your target. It simply takes time for you to overcome the fears of letting it go off line.

Eventually you will be comfortable with the sense of tuning into your inner image and letting your inner golfer play. You will find the trust needed to react to these images, and you will enjoy expressing your inner feelings through your play. As you become more and more comfortable with this process, you will be able to connect these experiences to your chosen target. Therefore, your play will once again become more precise. However, this precision will be expressed with a sense of freedom instead of control.

Since it's very difficult to truly capture this experience in words, I'll refrain from talking about it much further. For it's like hearing over and over that you're supposed to be patient and keep an even temperament on the golf course. Even though it sounds logical, it only hits home once you've experienced its true meaning. So, I'll leave this discussion of letting your inner golfer play with one last thought, *letting your inner golfer play is much more a state of being - an internal attitude you might say - than it is a physical happening.*

The Game

The game provides us many different opportunities to explore life's deeper meanings. In Michael Murphy's, *Golf In The Kingdom*, the character Shivas Irons states, *"Gowf is a place to practice fascination."* We all know this to be true. We're all captivated by the game. We've all experienced the illusive lure that keeps us coming back.

As I mentioned earlier in this book, *it begins with the first experience of having everything come together, and from that point on, the golfer's future is inevitably full of anticipation. For in the future the possibility exists that the swing, the ball, and the target will all meet within one majestic moment. For some it's much more than just a good shot, it's a mystical connexion that brings all the energies of the game together for one purpose. Those who experience this mystical lure encounter a sense of fulfillment, belonging, and happiness. Once experienced, there begins a search for mastering its execution. Furthermore, each player soon realizes that it's because of this mystical connexion that we're attracted to the game in the first place.*

For me this is the essence of the game, and I believe for many of you it's the case as well. But what else could be meant by, "Gowf is a place to practice fascination"? It might mean that the game provides us with the opportunity to delve into the deeper sides of ourselves. This can be experienced in those moments of extraordinary performance. These experiences may provide a doorway to the unknown. They may allow us to experience parts of our character that rarely show up anywhere else in life. It may mean the game illuminates the good in our personalities as well as the bad. You might say the game exposes the essence of who we are. It might mean all of these things. Whatever we believe the game's fascination to be, we must understand that the game challenges us to master ourselves as we play.

As we step out onto the golf course, we take our life out there with us. Some people think they can escape from the realities of life when playing golf. They soon find out that the game amplifies what's going on in their life. *Whatever the exact meaning, the importance of bringing it up is that we must first master ourselves if we're truly going to master our play.*

I know for myself that there's never anything wrong with my game. Either I have balance in my life and I play well, or there's imbalance in my life and I play poorly. Even though we may be able to distract ourselves from these imbalances for a short period of time, the game takes so long to play that our worries are sure to show themselves at some point during the round. Then look out for what comes next. For most, golf simply becomes an expression of how balanced our lives are. If we find mental, physical, and inner balance, then we tend to play well. If any suffer, then we struggle with our play.

Dealing with these trials is much of what the

game's fascination is all about. Those who believe in this fascination understand that golf can become much more than a game. If it's approached properly, it can become a way of life. It can become a portal into the mysteries of the unknown, or a vehicle into the mysteries of mastering ourselves. If this is the case, then any judgment of our play must be assessed over the long run, instead of on a day-to-day basis.

With all this in mind, I suggest you always play golf with the enjoyment of the game in mind. When playing, try to swing in whatever manner makes you most happy. If you do so, you may find that your best swings will show themselves frequently. When you go out to play, focus on having fun with the game, while maintaining an underlined commitment to your total approach.

To help acquire the feeling of this type of play, find out what makes you happy about playing. Find some sort of fascination with your play. Whether it's projecting your energy outward, whether it's enjoying friendships while we play, whether it's sinking into the competitive experience, or whether it's simply enjoying the day off, it's all up to you. Whatever fascination you find, remember that golf is a game. When you're out there playing, commit to the feeling of playing instead of working. If you're working at the game, you're working at it because you've yet to acquire the experience necessary to trust yourself out on the golf course. Therefore, before you go out to play, you must make a decision as to whether you are going to go out and play the game, or practice the game. If practicing, practice and forget about your score. If playing, play and forget about technique. In either case, have fun with it.

If you decide to go out and play, focus on what it feels like to play golf instead of simply hitting the ball around the course. Remember, the game is an ongoing process. Whatever happens on one shot, the exact opposite may happen on the next. *The true score of how you play is measured in how you feel about yourself and your play at the end of the day.* While adding up that score, assess the total experience instead of simply counting up the numbers. The next time you go out to play, I'd like you to try something. Pay attention to whether it feels like you're simply hitting the ball around, or whether it feels like you're *playing.* Imagine how little children play, and assess your play based on that image. On your good shots I'll bet you'll have a sense of playing. Everything will feel effortless and relaxed. However, your bad shots will be full of worries, doubts, and fears. They'll feel full of tension and much more like work. With these shots you'll feel like you're simply hitting at the ball instead of swinging your energy out into the playing field. Remember, the ball simply gets in the way of the swing and follows the path your energy travels. *To play the game, your energy must be projected outward into the playing field. So if you want to play the game, you need to focus more on where your energy is going, instead of where the little white ball is going.*

Chapter Nine
The Future Of The Game

Golf, An Ever-Evolving Game

To understand the future of the game, we must first understand the game's history. It's a history rich in tradition and honor. It started as a gentlemen's game, but evolved into a game for the masses. The game has captured the hearts of presidents and scholars, doctors and clergymen, carpenters and construction workers. In short, people from all walks of life, across all cultural boundaries have embraced the game. The game's growth and popularity have climbed steadily over the last 50 years.

Actually, that is an understatement. It has been more of an explosion. Consider the dramatic influence the game has made on our economy. The game is like a huge beacon drawing all to its allure. As the game has evolved through the ages, it has experienced many different changes. Although golf's ancestral ties are rooted as far back as the Roman Empire, its evolution has experienced the greatest changes during the last 75 to 80 years. The changes in equipment, course conditions, and culture have accelerated the game's evolution. Some may argue that this is true of civilization as well, and therefore the game of golf simply followed its influences.

You might say, the game's evolution is a type of blueprint, helping to map out the evolution of civilization itself. Whatever your beliefs might be, the game's outer evolution has come full circle. We can see this clearly in the development of the modern game, throughout the twentieth century.

As the modern game of golf has evolved from the early 1900's until today, we've observed many different styles of play, many different swing techniques, and many different methods of teaching. To understand the game's evolution over this period of time, we must understand how science, technology, philosophy, psychology, and culture have affected society. Since the game is truly played within the eye of the public, societal forces have had a major effect on the game's evolution.

While reviewing this evolution, we will divide the whole period into a few different eras, and briefly mention some of the era's influences that helped transform the game. These eras are the *Classic Era*, the *Modern Era*, the *Power Era*, and the *Renaissance Era*.

From1900 until the end of the 1930's lived the *Classic Era*. *Its main focus was that of having good form. This is mainly because golf was only accessible to the country club member. Within the prestigious environment of the country club, it was understood that a player's appearance and conduct were foremost. The accomplished golfer was required to play the role of a well-mannered individual with poise and good character. This meant he must possess all the qualities of good form. The qualities included Balance, Rhythm, Timing, Centeredness, and Effortlessness. The professional golfers of the day appeared to approach the game with great ease, and exemplified poetry in motion.* The players of the Classic Era were allowed to achieve these goals while using any method suitable to the task. Players who epitomize the Classic Era include Gene Sarazen, Bobby Jones, and Henry Cotton.

Gene Sarazen built his swing around his hands and grip, but used the late-hit procedure of the body player. Bobby Jones harnessed the power of his body by rotating freely throughout his swing. His arms and hands were allowed to naturally respond to the activity of the body. Even though Bobby Jones was a body swinger, he also advocated freedom of the hands. Henry Cotton believed that the game was played predominantly with the hands, and that proper hand action was the key to good ball striking skills. He is arguably the best hands player of all time. Whether the player chose to use his body, his hands, or a combination of the two, the player was allowed to pursue his own style as long as the player's technique was effective and illustrated good form.

From 1940 until about 1965, the game began to focus its attention on a different style of play. This was the **Modern Era**. Its players began spending more time practicing in an effort to develop a more technically sound swing. Precision and accuracy were the major concerns during play. Mechanical theory began to take its foothold in the lessons of the day. Players started focusing on the Plane of the Swing, and the Physics of Motion. Utilizing the larger muscles of the body became important, and the late-hit method (or late release of the hands and wrists) become much more popular. During the backswing, the main focal point became creating resistance in the right leg. This was to allow the player to develop more coil throughout his body. In short, the golfers of the Modern Era became more technically oriented then those of the Classic Era.

Byron Nelson is largely considered the father of the Modern Swing, while Ben Hogan was attributed with perfecting it. Sam Snead also played during this period, but he maintained the swinger's style of the Classic Era. I believe Sam Snead became history's best swinger while perfecting the Swinger's style in the Modern Era. His technique was flawless, versatile, and extremely natural to the human body. Reaching this level of perfection, Snead accomplished greater longevity then any other player to date. One other player who should be mentioned is Mickey Wright. Her technique lies somewhere between Ben Hogan's and Byron Nelson's. Her technique is simple, yet complete, and her ability to make the transition from the long swing to the short swing was just as good as either Nelson's or Hogan's.

One of the main reasons the game progressed to such a technical level was the large influence modern technology had on the world during this period. The United States was well out of the industrial age and quickly traveling through the age of technology. Advances in electronics, television, film, and computers were beginning to play a large role in our lives. The game of golf simply evolved with those influences.

The **Power Era** began with Jack Nicklaus in the early 1960's, although I've to believe Arnold Palmer's popularity and power must have laid the framework for such an acceptability of power golf over precision golf. With the popularity of Palmer and the dominance of Nicklaus, the average public embraced the game. During this era, from about 1966 to about 1980, golf was no longer restricted to the world of country clubs, where style and image reigned supreme. The everyday golfer became a major force. *Television brought these* golfers of mesmerizing power to everyone's living room. Besides power, individuality was also starting to become acceptable. This is truly evident in the styles of swings and diversity of personalities that were present on the tour in the 70's. Notwithstanding, the social structure of the United States was also changing at this time, and the attitudes of the public were becoming more outwardly expressive.

The swing's source of power became a lateral weight shift, with an aggressive driving of the knees and legs towards the target. However, because it was recommended that the player maintain his head as a stable swing center, the players of the Power Era quickly developed what was later coined "The Reverse C." This "Reverse C" was caused by trying to drive the legs forward while trying to keep the head behind the ball. The harder the player drove his legs and the further back the head stayed, the greater the player arched his back. By the end of the 1970's, multitudes of professionals as well as amateurs found themselves suffering from bad backs.

Even though the Power Era was tremendously exciting, and a huge boost for the game of golf, I recommend staying away from techniques that produced the "Reverse C." As a matter of fact, every professional who flourished during the Power Era, and continued to play successfully in the 1980's eventually made the changes necessary to alleviate the unneeded pressure of the "Reverse C" on the back.

By the early 1980's it was quite apparent that the techniques of the Power Era were in some way faulty. The main focus became curing the faults of Power Golf. Professional golfers began to seek out ways of reducing the amount of tension placed on the muscles of the back. Such instructors as Jimmy Ballard, Hank Haney, and David Leadbetter began focusing on straightening the back during the finish, and pivoting around a fixed axis, the spine. These early attempts at resolving the "Reverse C" problem produced more accurate ball strikers, but they also significantly reduced the amount of power the player could transfer through the ball.

So, those golfers who strove to maintain power tended to keep some of the "Reverse C." These attempts at solving the problems of the Power Era utilized some of the methods of both the Classic and Modern Eras. Therefore, we find many players developed what I call the Modern Classic Style of Swing. While reviving the methods of the past masters, the beginning of the 80's set a true Renaissance into motion - giving birth to the *Renaissance Era*.

By 1985, the full emphasis of the Renaissance Era

had taken force. From the late '80's until present, the golfing world has learned to blend the best qualities of each era. Today's Renaissance players strive to use the fundamentals to produce, store, and deliver power efficiently. They focus on creating a centered rotation, with a synchronized weight transfer and a connected arm swing. Renaissance players also realize they must maintain balance, rhythm, timing, and effortlessness. In order to complete this package, the Renaissance Player must learn how to distinguish his own unique physiological type, and then use it in as natural a manner as possible. Therefore, the true Renaissance Golfer incorporates the fundamentals of the Classic Era, the precision of the Modern Era, and the individuality of the Power Era.

A brief look at history will show that life in the United States took on a similar Renaissance throughout the '80's. Our society went from the freedom of the Sixties, to the individuality of the Seventies, to a more conservative view in the Eighties. We can see these influences in the styles of clothes we wore. The image of the hippie in the Sixties and the Funkadelic styles of the Seventies gave way to the Preppies of the Eighties, and the Yuppies of the Nineties, the last two being truly reminiscent of the styles of the Forties and Fifties.

As the Eighties came to an end, we came to realize the problems that existed in society as well as in our swings. We exhausted all our practical solutions, and realized we must reach much deeper if we were going to continue to go forward. As society has been taking on a much more global view in the 1990's, we've found a need to search inside ourselves for the answers. To create a new, more spiritual future for ourselves, we must get rid of all our old baggage, and take steps forward into the unknown. We learned that the more we try to hold onto the past, the more stagnant our lives become. In other words, we needed to stop passing the buck. So, the Nineties have been truly focused on establishing this inward journey, a journey full of uncertainty, as well as tremendous possibilities.

Finally, as we look beyond golf's present horizon, we'll begin to see a game with expanding possibilities. Such a vision is led by the player's imagination, and the power of the subconscious mind. Thus, the game of the future will both include the complete Renaissance package as well as the workings of Golf's Inner Game. The Renaissance Era focused mainly on completing the game's outer evolution, whereas the future will be focused on completing the game's inner evolution.

Without such balance between inner and outer, mind and body, you will never become completely satisfied with your game. The portal into the future lies within your inner being. To reach your full potential, you must learn how to express your inner perfection while being content with the fact that you play in a world that will never be ideal. Your future will be more concerned with expressing your inner golfer, with less dependence on your outer golfer.

We can already see this progression beginning. Its evolution is inevitable. With the onset of Sports Psychology, research in the world of Quantum Physics, and Holograms, we are continually learning more and more about the world's more subtle levels of energy. We're continually getting to the center of our world, and beginning to understand what horizons await us there. Michael Murphy brought this mystical journey to our attention with his best seller, *Golf In The Kingdom*; and Timothy Gallwey further clarified the inner and outer distinction in *The Inner Game of Golf*. Now it's our job to continue the quest for the type of game we know in our hearts we are truly capable of.

Above all, remember that golf is only a game, so have fun while you play. But, never forget that the game provides you the opportunity to expand your horizons.

"As we step out onto the golf course, we take our life out there with us. Some people think they can escape from the realities of life when playing golf. They soon find out that the game amplifies what's going on in their life. I know for myself that there's never anything wrong with my game. Either I have balance in my life and I play well, or there's imbalance in my life and I play poorly."

Chapter Ten
The Photo Album

In this chapter I am going to simply provide you with loose pictures and swing sequences that may provide you a new perspective on the game. In *Golf In The Kingdom*, there is a section where Shivas Irons shows Michael Murphy a collection of photographs. Those photos were taken from interesting angles, providing new perspectives on the game of golf. Maybe some of these photos will do the same for you.

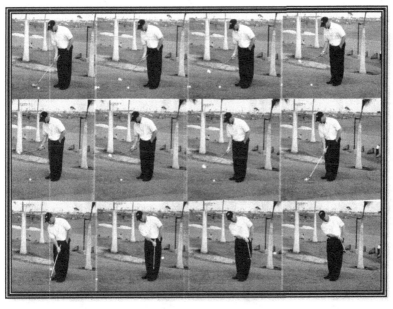

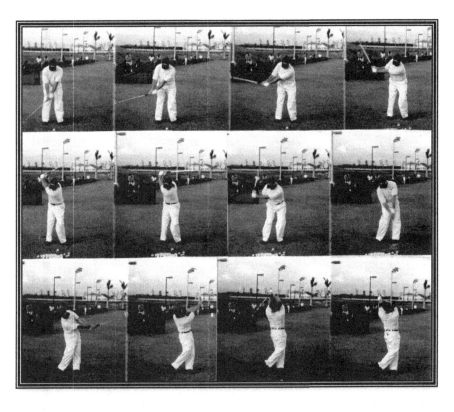

" The golfer as an individual knows that to give up on golf is to give up on one's self. For there is no one to blame, no matter what the circumstances. Whatever the future may hold, each player seeks out the most noble vision of the game, a vision full of possibility, and extraordinary achievement. In the end, the students who have the resolve to adventure beyond the traditional barriers of the game will find the freedom to reach their vision's full potential. For many it will become a way of life:"

The Way Of The Golfer - *Searching For New Horizons*

Your journey has just begun. Enjoy the adventure.

The Way Of The Golfer – Searching For New Horizons is just part of EA Tischler's New Horizons Golf Approach. The complete approach is organized into 4 stages. Stage One – Developing Your Fundamentals. Stage Two is about applications and techniques. Stage Three covers your biomechanics and Stage Four is about playing the game.

The approach is organized to help golfers of all skill levels achieve their goals. Whether beginner, avid golfer or professional you are certain to find the answers you are looking for within the New Horizons Golf Approach.

NEW HORIZONS GOLF

A JOURNEY INTO THE EXPERIENCE

Inquire about New Horizons Golf Schools that cover Mastering Putting, Fore54 Stroke Saving Skills, The Fundamentals, Impact Dynamics, Power Stacking and Power-of-3 Golf Biomechanics. Visit www.newhorizonsgolf.com to find out where you can attend one of our schools.

EA Tischler is the Founder and Director of Instruction of the New Horizons Golf Approach. He grew up in California's San Francisco Bay Area. He attended U.C. San Diego where he was the golf team captain. In 1989 he turned professional, and has been playing and coaching ever since. In 1992 he was injured and stopped play for four years. In 1994 he moved to Hawaii where he became known as the "Pro's-Pro." In 2000 Ed was voted as one of Hawaii's top teachers in the August issue of Golf Digest Magazine. As a player he has compiled 8 hole-in-ones, 2 double-eagles and played to +4.5 handicap. As a professional coach he has written 18 golf instructional books, invented and patented a variety of training aids and is the founder of the New Horizons Golf Approach. To contact EA Tischler, e-mail him at newhorizonsgolfer@yahoo.com. You can find more information about the New Horizons Golf Approach at www.newhorizonsgolf.com.